I listened to the Military Doctor who lied!

I listened to the Military General who lied!

David Langtry

This book is based on Former Classification Officer Terry Mallenby's recollections, supplemented by Personal Federal Court documents.

Terry Mallenby, BA, BSW, MA
Former Classification Officer
B.C. Maximum Security Penitentiary
Canadian Penitentiary Service
New Westminster, Canada

Index   **Page**

Appendices

Chapter 1

The "Mean-Spirited" Nature of the Federal Government of Canada!

This book is not about the average soldier, the "grunt", as they are affectionately called.

The author finds the protest of some profs at the University of Regina against Project Hero absolutely deplorable [see Appendix 1].

This book is rather about the miserable treatment of 'the little guy'.

Where does this "mean-spirited" attitude come from?

Let's look at the "mean-spirited" nature of the Federal Government of Canada to prove the point.

What kind of money are the Canadian politicians "raking in".

As cited, here are some of the salaries of politicians at a federal level:

"Backbench Member of Parliament (MP): $157,731

MP with odd job appointments (ie. caucus chair, commitee chairman etc): $163,415 – $196,910

Leader of Federal Party: $211,425

Junior Cabinet Minister (ie. ministers/secretaries of state): $214,368

Senior Cabinet Minister/Opposition Leader/Speaker of the House: $233,247 + car allowances

Prime Minister: $315,462 + large house budget + car allowances"[1]

However, what did the Government of Canada recently award Canadian seniors with?

As cited by Claude Gravelle, an NDP MP for Nickel Belt (Ontario):

"Mr. Speaker, seniors are greatly worried about the coming winter. Many are on fixed income and are very worried about paying their bills. To add insult to injury, the government only gave a $1.50 increase to the old age security."[2]

As further cited by Claude Gravelle:

"The Conservative government can spare millions of dollars on television and billboard ads but can only spare a $1.50 increase to old age security, after a two year freeze. [3]

What?

With these Federal politicians feeding at "the trough", they miserly give Canadian seniors a lousy $1.50 increase after a two year freeze on their meager income?

Who heads the Canadian Conservative Government, Stephen Harper, Prime Minister of Canada, Hill Office, House of Commons, Ottawa, Ontario, Canada K1A 0A6; Telephone: (613) 992-4211; Fax: (613) 941-6900; EMail: Harper.S@parl.gc.ca.

If you think this unfair, why not give him a call, fax him or email him?

The Canadian Government may not realize a meager $1.50 raise after three years is not "scrooge" like?

Another guy you might want to communicate with is: Jim Flaherty, Minister of Finance, Hill Office, House of Commons, Ottawa, Ontario, Canada K1A 0A6; Telephone: (613) 992-6344; Fax: (613) 992-8320; EMail: Flaherty.J@parl.gc.ca.

Then again, you might want to contact this one: Diane Ablonczy, Minister of State (Seniors), Hill Office, House of Commons, Ottawa, Ontario, Canada K1A 0A6; Telephone: (613) 996-2756; Fax: (613) 992-2537; EMail: Ablonczy.D@parl.gc.ca.

What is a senior's pension?

An Old Age Security Pension appears to be $521.62 per month. [4]

Oh, my God.

A whole $521.62 per month?

Almost $6,000.00 per year [old age is taxed, isn't it]?

What Canadian Minister is responsible for this "wind-fall"?

Why, apparently she is Diane Finley?

You may definitely want to communicate with this one, unless you think the $1.50 raise after three years isn't mean-spirited?

Diane Finley, Minister of Human Resources Development (Services Canada), Hill Office, House of Commons, Ottawa, Ontario, Canada K1A 0A6; Telephone: (613) 996-4974; Fax: (613) 996-9749; EMail: Finley.D@parl.gc.ca

What kind of people are these Canadian politicians, a quick web search found these comments.

Let's look at the captain of the ship, Harper. As cited in The Hill Times:

"Prime Minister Stephen Harper took steps Thursday to trim expenses in the federal civil service, eliminate the per vote subsidy for federal political parties, and other belt-tightening 'lead by example' measures, but Mr. Harper also opted for the more costly position of naming 11 ministers of state over the less costly position of secretaries of state when he unveiled his much larger 38-member ministry on Oct. 30."[5]

There are 11 ministers of state serving in the Conservative government's ministry. While ministers of state are not technically members of Cabinet, they are members of the ministry, and the combined cost of the $74,000 pay increase for the 11 ministers of state is $818,400. The total operating budgets for ministers of state can be up to $642,590, which could potentially bring budgetary expenses for the 11 new ministers of state to $7,068,490, or $7,711,080 with the minister of state salaries.[6]

Yep, that seems fair, doesn't it?

Give the Canadian seniors a $1.50 raise after three years but spend over 7 million on a more expensive ministry.

Boy, does the "the trough" look pretty good to Harper, what do you think?

Now, let's look at Flaherty. As cited:

"The Canadian Federation of Independent Business has lashed out at the federal government for granting wage increases to public servants at the same time Canadians are being told to brace for a period of frugality."[7]

"We are stunned to learn of this tentative deal which is completely contradictory to the messages the federal government has been giving —

warning Canadians that we are in an era of modest growth and that we all need to tighten our belts," CFIB's president, Catherine Swift, said in an open letter to Prime Minister Stephen Harper, Treasury Board President Stockwell Day and Finance Minister Jim Flaherty. [8]

"Are we to understand that the federal public servants who already enjoy a significant wage and benefit premium of over 40 per cent, on average, over their private sector counterparts are being permitted to play by different rules than the rest of us?" [9]

Hmmm, tell the rest of people in Canada to "tighten their belt" but let's give ourselves a raise?

Is that what these comments are about?

Let's look at Ablonczy. As reported:

The Honorable Diane Ablonczy, Minister of State for Seniors, today (June 15, 2010) pledged the Government's support in the fight against elder abuse at the World Elder Abuse Awareness Day conference in Toronto. [10]

"Any form of abuse is unacceptable and should not be tolerated. We need to create an environment where people will take action against this serious issue," said Minister of State Ablonczy. "We need to give seniors and other Canadians the information they need to raise awareness, stand up and take action." [11]

Hello, hello – anyone home?

What could be more damaging to a senior than being given a $1.50 raise after three years?

Did Ablonczy who is supposed to be looking out for Canadian seniors raise any protest when their meager income was frozen in year one?

Did Ablonczy who is supposed to be looking out for Canadian seniors raise any protest when their meager income was frozen in year two?

Did Ablonczy who is supposed to be looking out for Canadian seniors raise any protest when their meager income was given a whole $1.50 increase in year three?

It has to be asked, is this Ablonczy "out to lunch too"?

Let's look at Findley. As cited:

The Harper gang are "hogs at the trough" they used to complain about. [12]

As reported by Bob Speller, federal Liberal candidate for Haldimand-Norfolk:

"The husband of local MP Diane Finley is set to make $130,000 a year for life courtesy of the Harper government." [13]

"Haldimand-Norfolk's farmers and steelworkers are struggling but Ms Finley's husband is getting cash for life," Speller said. [14]

"Diane Finley's husband has won the lottery and we are all going to pay for it." he said. [15]

As further cited by Bob Speller:

"Stephen Harper is now officially the Senate patronage king. Harper used to say he would never appoint his friends to the Senate but as Prime Minister, Harper brazenly stacked the Senate with 18 appointments just before Christmas. Now he is poised to do it again just before Labour Day." [16]

"He has now tied Conservative Robert Borden as the only Prime Minister in Canadian history to make 26 Senate appointments in a single year." [17]

Diane Finley's and the Conservative Party's web site said during the 2006 election that "A conservative government will not appoint to the Senate anyone who does not have a mandate for the people". Just another one of the numerous broken promises from this Member of Parliament Speller said. [18]

"The difference between the Harper gang and hogs at the trough is that hogs will stop feeding when the trough is empty. The trough will never empty for the Harper gang and we will all pay for it." [19]

Footnotes

1. Federal Politician Salaries – Higher Than You Think
Written by FrugalTrader on Oct 5, 2009 filed under General Finance

2 – 3. Hansard, 40th Parliament, 3rd session, Number 075, Friday,

October 1, 2010

Also cited at: Claude Gravelle, an NDP MP for Nickel Belt (Ontario)

4. Old Age Security Benefit Payment Rates, October - December 2010

5 – 6. The Hill Times
April 14th, 2010 by Harris MacLeod

7 - 9. Business group slams public service wage hikes
Deal contradicts message Tories have been sending, CFIB says
Last Updated: Wednesday, October 6, 2010 | 2:33 PM ET .

10 – 11. Minister of State Ablonczy marks World Elder Abuse
Awareness Day. Toronto, Ontario, Canada; June 15, 2010

12 – 19. Senate appointment means Finley's husband "wins lottery" with
"cash for life" Bob Speller

Chapter 2

The "mean-spirited" nature of the Government of Canada can be seen in this case of the "clown sized" boots!

In this case, a young Canadian Forces female member who was quite willing to serve in spite of the harassment females suffer in the Canadian Military [see Appendix 2a, 2b, 2c & 2d] and in spite of the absolute stupid deadly gaffes by the Canadian Force Commanders [see Appendix 3].

Instead, she was treated like dirt.

In spite of this young Canadian Forces female member's enthusiasm to join the Canadian Forces, her dad knew immediately there was something wrong with the outfit or at least some of the people in the outfit [see Appendix 3].

For example, when the Canadian Government and the Canadian Forces knew they would be sending the fine sons and daughters into harms way in a desert campaign, they were either too stupid or too cheap to equip them with proper colored flack jackets [see Appendix 3].

Instead of desert beige, the fine sons and daughters were sent into harms way with bright jolly green colors [see Appendix 3]?

What?

The author can see it now, prior to deployment, the politicians and the Canadian Force Commanders reviewing the troops on parade in their jolly green flack jackets – and the politicians and the Canadian Force Commanders probably saying amongst themselves – don't our troops look grand, their jolly green flack jackets match the lush green foliage of the trees lining the parade grounds?

The author had to ask; is this the usual logic of some in the Canadian Forces?

If yes, it's just plain stupid … and deadly?

In fact, if it wasn't so deadly to those first troops on the ground in Afghanistan, it would be comical.

Lucky for our troops, the American military came equipped and lent our sons and daughters proper colored desert beige flack jackets.

Continuing, we'll see later in this book the apparent fabrication ["lies"] against this young Canadian Forces female member to support the actions against her.

After all, it's apparently obvious the Canadian Military is not above lying or covering up [see Appendix 4a, 4b & 4c].

It is also about the departments that blocked justice for her.

And, it's about the individuals that concluded plantar fasciitis discrimination is "frivolous" according to this human rights department?

The conclusion, what a colossal waste of time putting in an internal grievance against the Canadian Forces?

What a colossal waste of time complaining to the Canadian Government about discrimination?

Both apparently support the Canadian Forces at the expense of, in this case, this 'little gal'?.

Chapter 3

Major foot problems at BMQ due to improperly fitted boots by Comm Unit - The Case of the Clown Sized Boots!

It all started one day when this young female was looking for a way to pay for her college education.

She saw an advertisement in the local paper to join the local Reserve Unit where she lived.

She applied to the 748 Communications Unit in Nanaimo, British Columbia, Canada.

She passed the testing and physical and was considered suitable [see Appendix 5a & 5b].

She was now a member of the Canadian Forces.

Her references were good [as an example, see Appendix 6], and whatever she lacked in confidence would surely be corrected with a little military training, at least that's what was thought.

However, no sooner was she in the Nanaimo 748 Communications Unit, she noticed her boots didn't fit [See cover of this book and Appendix 7].

After all, this young Canadian Forces female member had spend 4 years in Air Cadets with proper fitting boots and she well knew a proper fitting boot from the idiotic boot this Comm Unit was trying to pawn off on her [see Appendix 7].

In spite of her attempts to correct the problem, she was sent to "boot camp" [Canada's BMQ] with these boots.

Even Canada's General W.Z. Natynczyk on page 3 of his letter dated 29 January, 2010 confirmed that "I find that the boot fitting procedures set out in the supply manual were not followed by supply personnel at 748 Comm Sqn, Nanaimo" [See Appendix 23].

Surprise, surprise what do you think happened, when she turned up at "boot camp" in these grossly oversized "clown sized" boots?

You guessed it, major foot problems interfering with her doing well on the BMQ.

Even General W.Z. Natynczyk again on page 3 of his letter dated 29 January, 2010 confirmed the importance of proper fitting boots, "improper fitted footwear affects the general well-being of an individual, often to such an extent as to impair health, morale and efficiency. It is, therefore, of the utmost importance that individuals wear footwear for which they have been measured and properly fitted" [See Appendix 23].

Apparently, a black and white case, one would think?

Not in Canada apparently?

As such, the rest of the book highlights the apparent fabrication(s) ["lies"], the refusal to accommodate, and the refusal that any discrimination had taken place.

Most of the information in this book comes from Access to Information sources.

Chapter 3 [Major foot problems at BMQ due to improperly fitted boots by Comm Unit]

You can imagine turning up at "boot camp" with these "clown sized" boots and expected to perform tough physical activity [see Appendix 7].

In any event, this young Canadian Forces female member turned up at "boot camp" in July, 2006.

Surprise, surprise ... soon after, on 05 July, 2006 the medical unit at Shilo Manitoba base camp recorded "blisters and hot spots" on left and right foot -- Signed by Canadian Forces Shilo Base Surgeon Major Salsman [See Appendix 8].

Also recorded in the medical unit at Shilo Manitoba base camp on 05 July, 2006 "on left foot there is a 1" long friction mark on the posterior aspect of the foot slightly proximal from the 'calcaneus(?)'. There is also a blister on the plantar aspect of the foot located on the heel. It appears to be relatively deep. On the right foot there is a similar friction mark as described on the left foot. There are hot spots located on the bottom of both heels" -- Signed by Canadian Forces Shilo Base Surgeon Major Salsman [see Appendix 8].

As also recorded in the medical unit at Shilo Manitoba base camp on 05 July, 2006 "friction marks, hot spots and blisters caused by grossly oversized combat boots" -- Signed by Canadian Forces Shilo Base Surgeon Major Salsman [see Appendix 8].

As also recorded in the medical unit at Shilo Manitoba base camp on 05 July, 2006 "enquire about new boots, should be fitted with orthotics, and dressed friction marks, dressed with 'hypafix(?)' and 'mepore(?)' -- Signed by Canadian Forces Shilo Base Surgeon Major Salsman [see Appendix 8].

It was also at this time that Canadian Forces Shilo Base Surgeon Major Salsman gave this young Canadian Forces female member a pamphlet on plantar fasciitis [see Appendix 9].

Also recorded   in the medical unit at Shilo Manitoba base camp on 05 July, 2006 specific instructions that this young Canadian Forces female member should not drill, not march, not run, and no ruck or webbing marches [see Appendix 10].

Good God, how on earth could this young Canadian Forces female member pass the BMQ if her feet were so bad because of the idiotic "grossly oversized combat boots" fitted her by her 748 Communications Unit?

After all, remember it was Canada's General W.Z. Natynczyk on page 3 of his letter dated 29 January, 2010 who confirmed that "I find that the boot fitting procedures set out in the supply manual were not followed by supply personnel at 748 Comm Sqn, Nanaimo" [See Appendix 23].

In addition, as also recorded in the medical unit at Shilo Manitoba base camp on 05 July, 2006 specific instructions that this young Canadian Forces female member should "wear running shoes until member receives proper fitting boots" [see Appendix 10].

However, these "Einstein's" apparently didn't realize that wearing running shoes also apparently increases the pain and damage caused by plantar fasciitis. As cited[1]:

"Anthony (1987)[2] reported that running shoes should be considered protective devices (from dangerous or painful objects) rather than corrective devices, as their capacity for shock absorption and control of over-pronation is limited."[3]

"The modern running shoe and footwear generally reduce sensory feedback, apparently without diminishing injury-inducing impact–a process Robbins and Gouw (1991)[4] described as the "perceptual illusion" of athletic footwear."[5]

"A resulting false sense of security may contribute to the risk of injury (Robbins and Gouw, 1991)."[6]

What conclusion(s) were reached if one wore running shoes?

As cited:

"Running in shoes appears to increase the risk of plantar fasciitis and other chronic injuries of the lower limb by modifying the transfer of shock to muscles and supporting structures."[7]

Good God, again how on earth could this young Canadian Forces female member pass the BMQ if she couldn't slog it out in the mud and terrain doing the physical aspects of the course, the marches, etc.

Again, as recorded on 07 July, 2006 specific instructions for this young Canadian Forces female member indicated she should not drill, not march, and no ruck or webbing marches and this time no prolonged standing for more than 20 minutes [see Appendix 11].

Good God, again how on earth could this young Canadian Forces female member pass the BMQ if she couldn't stand for more than 20 minutes – any parade activity sometimes takes hours of standing?

On 10 July, 2006 Canadian Forces Shilo Base Surgeon Major Salsman placed an order for special proper fitting boots for this young Canadian Forces female member with "vibram-soles" to accommodate her wide feet so she could perform her military duties [see Appendix 12].

Even General W.Z. Natynczyk again on page 3 of his letter dated 29 January, 2010 confirmed the importance of proper fitting boots, "improper fitted footwear affects the general well being of an individual, often to such an extent as to impair health, morale and efficiency. It is, therefore, of the utmost importance that individuals wear footwear for which they have been measured and properly fitted" [See Appendix 23].

The end result, this young Canadian Forces female member was taken from her BMQ course and admitted to Brandon Regional Health Centre on 13 July, 2006 with an infected toe because of the grossly oversized boots she had been issued by my 748 Comm unit "area around blister reddened … pus" [see Appendix 13].

Finally, as recorded in the medical unit at Shilo Manitoba base camp on 14 July, 2006 it indicated that this young Canadian Forces female member had been "in emergency last night" and then referred to a "blister infected right foot" [see Appendix 14].

This young Canadian Forces female member was prescribed an antibiotic for her infected foot [see Appendix 15].

This young Canadian Forces female member was recommended for a medical RTU [return to unit] at 07:23 on 14 July, 2006 [see Appendix 16].

Then again this young Canadian Forces female member was recommended for a medical RTU [return to unit] at 15:15 on 14 July, 2006 [see Appendix 17].

Footnotes

1. Barefoot Running
Michael Warburton

2. Anthony RJ (1987). The functional anatomy of the running training shoe. Chiropodist, December, 451-459

3. Barefoot Running
Michael Warburton

4. Robbins SE, Gouw GJ (1991). Athletic footwear: unsafe due to perceptual illusions. Medicine and Science in Sports and Exercise 23, 217-224

5 - 7. Barefoot Running
Michael Warburton

Chapter 4

Is this the first "lie" by Canadian Forces Shilo Base Surgeon Major Salsman?

Let's review this case so far.

On 05 July, 2006 the medical unit at Shilo Manitoba base camp recorded "blisters and hot spots" on left and right foot -- Signed by Canadian Forces Shilo Base Surgeon Major Salsman [See Appendix 8].

Also recorded in the medical unit at Shilo Manitoba base camp on 05 July, 2006 "on left foot there is a 1" long friction mark on the posterior aspect of the foot slightly proximal from the 'calcaneus(?)'. There is also a blister on the plantar aspect of the foot located on the heel. It appears to be relatively deep. On the right foot there is a similar friction mark as described on the left foot. There are hot spots located on the bottom of both heels" -- Signed by Canadian Forces Shilo Base Surgeon Major Salsman [see Appendix 8].

As also recorded in the medical unit at Shilo Manitoba base camp on 05 July, 2006 "friction marks, hot spots and blisters caused by grossly oversized combat boots" -- Signed by Canadian Forces Shilo Base Surgeon Major Salsman [see Appendix 8].

As also recorded in the medical unit at Shilo Manitoba base camp on 05 July, 2006 "enquire about new boots, should be fitted with orthotics, and dressed friction marks, dressed with 'hypafix(?)' and 'mepore(?)' -- Signed by Canadian Forces Shilo Base Surgeon Major Salsman [see Appendix 8].

It was also at this time that Canadian Forces Shilo Base Surgeon Major Salsman gave this young Canadian Forces female member a pamphlet on plantar fasciitis [see Appendix 9].

On 10 July, 2006 Canadian Forces Shilo Base Surgeon Major Salsman placed an order for special proper fitting boots for this young Canadian Forces female member with "vibram-soles" to accommodate her wide feet so she could perform her military duties [see Appendix 12].

It should also be noted, as we will see later in this book, this young Canadian Forces female member was never issued these specially ordered boots.

The end result, this young Canadian Forces female member was taken from her BMQ course and admitted to Brandon Regional Health Centre on 13 July, 2006 with an infected toe because of the "grossly oversized" boots she had been issued by my 748 Comm unit with indication that the "area around blister reddened … pus" [see Appendix 13].

Finally, as recorded in the medical unit at Shilo Manitoba base camp on 14 July, 2006 it indicated that this young Canadian Forces female member had been "in emergency last night" and then referred to a "blister infected right foot" [see Appendix 14].

This young Canadian Forces female member was prescribed an antibiotic for her infected foot [see Appendix 15].

This young Canadian Forces female member was recommended for a medical RTU [return to unit] at 07:23 on 14 July, 2006 [see Appendix 16] and again recommended for a medical RTU [return to unit] at 15:15 on 14 July, 2006 [see Appendix 17].

Even Canadian Forces Shilo Base Surgeon Major Salsman on 14 July, 2006 recommended this young Canadian Forces female member be medically RTU'd: "on 14 July, the Base Surgeon recommended [this young Canadian Forces female member] for medical RTU" [see Appendix 18].

Everyone got that straight so far?

Seems quite straight foreword, doesn't it?

That is, until you get to an apparent "cover-up" letter dated 17 July, 2006 written by none other than Canadian Forces Shilo Base Surgeon Major Salsman [see Appendix 19].

In it, Canadian Forces Shilo Base Surgeon Major Salsman says "I am unsure what is wrong with this lady" [see Appendix 19].

What?

Didn't this guy read his own medical notes before he wrote this letter?

Can anyone spell fabrication ["lie"]?

Seems clear to me?

What about you?

It was quite clear that Canadian Forces Shilo Base Surgeon Major Salsman letter dated 17 July, 2006 was apparently to undo the recommendation on 14 July, 2006 that this young Canadian Forces female member be medically RTU'd to her unit [see Appendices 16 & 17].

Incredibly too, it was quite clear that Canadian Forces Shilo Base Surgeon Major Salsman letter dated 17 July, 2006 was apparently to undo his own recommendation on 14 July, 2006 that this young Canadian Forces female member be medically RTU'd to her unit [see Appendix 18].

If this young Canadian Forces female member was medically RTU'd to her unit, they would have had to issue her the special boots ordered on 10 July, 2006 by Base Surgeon Major Salsman and they would have to let her try the BMQ again.

After all, due to the severe medical problems caused by the "grossly oversized boots" issued by her 748 Comm Unit [see Appendix 8], this young Canadian Forces female member was unable to complete the majority of the BMQ course [see Appendix 20].

Specifically, as cited, she was unable to complete "Survive under NBC conditions" or the "Field training" nor the "Drills" and neither the "Service rifle" [see Appendix 20].

Give her another chance?

No, that's apparently not in Canadian Forces' vocabulary.

Let's 'screw her over' -- ah, does that appear to fit Canadian Forces' philosophy much better?

If Canadian Forces Shilo Base Surgeon Major Salsman could undo his own medical RTU recommendation given on 14 July, 2006 [see Appendices 16, 17 & 18] to a simple RTU, her unit would have to do nothing for her.

So apparently the game became, let's swallow one's ethics and write some apparent "cover-up" letter, such as the one Base Surgeon Major Salsman wrote on 17 July, 2006 [see Appendix 19]?

Oh, guess what -- that's apparently what he did [see Appendix 19]?

Chapter 5

Some thoughts about liars!

Sort of reminds the author about liars?

The nice thing about liars, they commit more and more lies trying to protect themselves?

Eventually the lies become obvious?

Ask any good police detective.

That's how cases are solved.

Sort of reminds the author of these cases.

In one case, "a Yellowknife man whose leg was broken during an arrest outside a bar has been found not guilty of assaulting a police officer and obstructing justice."[1]

In fact, Chief Judge Brian Bruser, in his decision released last month, said RCMP [Royal Canadian Mounted Police] Const. Scot Newberry attacked Devon Herback, not the other way around.[2]

"There is no doubt that what occurred was excessive force in the course of an unlawful arrest," Bruser wrote.[3]

"Newberry said Herback resisted arrest and tried to kick him, but Bruser found Newberry was the aggressor."[4]

"The judge said in his ruling he did not believe Newberry's version of events that night. "His evidence was frequently vague, evasive, implausible or simply unbelievable or unreliable."[5]

In one more situation, RCMP Cpl. Andre Turcotte was found guilty of the assault on Scott Campbell in Penticton.[6]

The beating left the man unconscious on the side of Highway 97 in Summerland near the Sumac Ridge turnoff on Nov. 29, 2007.[7]

Judge Dev Dley said Turcotte punched Campbell and eventually landed "at least three kicks," to Campbell before an oncoming car stopped.[8]

What did RCMP Turcotte do?

He left the scene?

"It was then Turcotte jumped into his vehicle and left the unconscious man and the witnesses."[9]

"What he did was intentional and inexcusable ... the nature of the assault can only be described as brutal," said Dley adding Turcotte breached his trust with the public.[10]

"Dley found that Turcotte intentionally hid that he had been involved in the incident from a fellow officer when asked about it the following day."[11]

He also called Turcotte's eventual statement to RCMP "misleading," and other inconsistencies led the judge to take the victims word over Turcotte's.[12]

Wow!

Holey, smokes?

If members of the Royal Canadian Mounted Police apparently lie[13], it would seem that some other employees of the Canadian Government are apparently equally able to lie too?

Could this be true?

Would this include some members of the Canadian Forces?

The apparent "cover-up" letter, such as the one Base Surgeon Major Salsman wrote on 17 July, 2006 [see Appendix 19], would seem to indicate the affirmative?

Wouldn't it?

Just to make sure, let's review the facts as revealed apparently by Base Surgeon Major Salsman's own hand?

On 05 July, 2006 the medical unit at Shilo Manitoba base camp recorded "blisters and hot spots" on left and right foot -- Signed by Canadian Forces Shilo Base Surgeon Major Salsman [See Appendix 8].

Also recorded in the medical unit at Shilo Manitoba base camp on 05 July, 2006 "on left foot there is a 1" long friction mark on the posterior aspect of the foot slightly proximal from the 'calcaneus(?)'. There is also a blister on the plantar aspect of the foot located on the heel. It appears to be relatively deep. On the right foot there is a similar friction mark as described on the left foot. There are hot spots located on the bottom of both heels" -- Signed by Canadian Forces Shilo Base Surgeon Major Salsman [see Appendix 8].

As also recorded in the medical unit at Shilo Manitoba base camp on 05 July, 2006 "friction marks, hot spots and blisters caused by grossly oversized combat boots" -- Signed by Canadian Forces Shilo Base Surgeon Major Salsman [see Appendix 8].

As also recorded in the medical unit at Shilo Manitoba base camp on 05 July, 2006 "enquire about new boots, should be fitted with orthotics, and dressed friction marks, dressed with 'hypafix(?)' and 'mepore(?)' -- Signed by Canadian Forces Shilo Base Surgeon Major Salsman [see Appendix 8].

On 10 July, 2006 Canadian Forces Shilo Base Surgeon Major Salsman placed an order for special proper fitting boots for this young Canadian Forces female member with "vibram-soles" to accommodate her wide feet so she could perform her military duties [see Appendix 12].

The Brandon Regional Health Centre on 13 July, 2006 with an infected toe because of the "grossly oversized" boots she had been issued by my 748 Comm unit with indication that the "area around blister reddened ... pus" [see Appendix 13].

As recorded in the medical unit at Shilo Manitoba base camp on 14 July, 2006 it indicated that this young Canadian Forces female member had been "in emergency last night" and then referred to a "blister infected right foot" [see Appendix 14].

This young Canadian Forces female member was prescribed an antibiotic for her infected foot [see Appendix 15].

This young Canadian Forces female member was recommended for a medical RTU [return to unit] at 07:23 on 14 July, 2006 [see Appendix 16] and again recommended for a medical RTU [return to unit] at 15:15 on 14 July, 2006 [see Appendix 17].

Even Canadian Forces Shilo Base Surgeon Major Salsman on 14 July, 2006 recommended this young Canadian Forces female member be medically RTU'd: "on 14 July, the Base Surgeon recommended [this young Canadian Forces female member] for medical RTU" [see Appendix 18].

Again, has everyone got that straight so far?

Again, it seems quite straight foreword, doesn't it?

That is, until you get to an apparent "cover-up" letter dated 17 July, 2006 written by none other than Canadian Forces Shilo Base Surgeon Major Salsman [see Appendix 19]?

In it, Canadian Forces Shilo Base Surgeon Major Salsman says "I am unsure what is wrong with this lady" [see Appendix 19]?

What?

As mentioned, didn't this guy read his own medical notes before he wrote this letter?

As asked, can anyone spell fabrication ["lie"]?

Footnotes

1 - 5. RCMP Officer criticized for arrest. Canadian Press. Tuesday, February 15, 2005.

6 - 12. RCMP officer sentenced for assault. By Kristi Patton - Penticton Western News. Published: June 01, 2010, Updated: June 01, 2010.

13. Also reference to: The Very Thin Red Line: This police force is "horribly broken". Amazon.com

Chapter 6

Let's look at Canadian Forces Shilo Base Surgeon Major Salsman's letter a little closer to see what other lies it contains?

Let's have another look at that apparent "cover-up" letter dated 17 July, 2006 written by none other than Canadian Forces Shilo Base Surgeon Major Salsman [see Appendix 19]?

In it, Canadian Forces Shilo Base Surgeon Major Salsman says "I am unsure what is wrong with this lady" [see Appendix 19]?

We've already seen, unless this guy is "a blithering idiot" and had forgotten about his own personal involvement with this young Canadian Forces female member [see Chapter 3] that his statement "I am unsure what is wrong with this lady" was apparently an outright fabrication ["lie"]?

What else does Canadian Forces Shilo Base Surgeon Major Salsman say in his 17 July, 2006 letter [see Appendix 19]?

Salsman goes on to state: "There were almost daily (seven visits in 10 days) visits for a variety of vague yet disturbing physical complaints"?

Hey "Einstein", ever hear of this cited by General W.Z. Natynczyk on page 3 of his letter dated 29 January, 2010 emphasizing the importance of proper fitting boots, "improper fitted footwear affects the general well being of an individual, often to such an extent as to impair health, morale and efficiency. It is, therefore, of the utmost importance that individuals wear footwear for which they have been measured and properly fitted" [See Appendix 23].

Hey guy, you saw the "Clown Sized" boots this young Canadian Forces female member had been issued [see Appendix 7].

You even referred to the size of her boots yourself?

Specifically, as also recorded in the medical unit at Shilo Manitoba base camp on 05 July, 2006 "friction marks, hot spots and blisters caused by grossly oversized combat boots" -- Signed by Canadian Forces Shilo Base Surgeon Major Salsman [see Appendix 8].

You even spelled out what you now call her "vague physical complaints"?

On 05 July, 2006 the medical unit at Shilo Manitoba base camp recorded "blisters and hot spots" on left and right foot -- Signed by Canadian Forces Shilo Base Surgeon Major Salsman [See Appendix 8].

You again spelled out what you now call her "vague physical complaints"?

Also recorded in the medical unit at Shilo Manitoba base camp on 05 July, 2006 "on left foot there is a 1" long friction mark on the posterior aspect of the foot slightly proximal from the 'calcaneus(?)'. There is also a blister on the plantar aspect of the foot located on the heel. It appears to be relatively deep. On the right foot there is a similar friction mark as described on the left foot. There are hot spots located on the bottom of both heels" -- Signed by Canadian Forces Shilo Base Surgeon Major Salsman [see Appendix 8].

You yet again spelled out what you now call her "vague physical complaints"?

As also recorded in the medical unit at Shilo Manitoba base camp on 05 July, 2006 "enquire about new boots, should be fitted with orthotics, and dressed friction marks, dressed with 'hypafix(?)' and 'mepore(?)' -- Signed by Canadian Forces Shilo Base Surgeon Major Salsman [see Appendix 8].

One more time, you even spelled out what you now call her "vague physical complaints"?

It was also at this time that Canadian Forces Shilo Base Surgeon Major Salsman gave this young Canadian Forces female member a pamphlet on plantar fasciitis [see Appendix 9].

And finally, you again even spelled out what you now call her "vague physical complaints"?

On 10 July, 2006 Canadian Forces Shilo Base Surgeon Major Salsman placed an order for special proper fitting boots for this young Canadian Forces female member with "vibram-soles" to accommodate her wide feet so she could perform her military duties [see Appendix 12].

Ah, what's that word that comes to mind when one reads that apparent "cover-up" letter dated 17 July, 2006 written by Canadian Forces Shilo Base Surgeon Major Salsman [see Appendix 19]?

Ah yes, can anyone spell fabrication ["lie"]?

Chapter 7

Let's have another look at Canadian Forces Shilo Base Surgeon Major Salsman's letter to see what other lies it contains?

Let's look at that apparent "cover-up" letter dated 17 July, 2006 written by none other than Canadian Forces Shilo Base Surgeon Major Salsman one more time [see Appendix 19]?

In it, Canadian Forces Shilo Base Surgeon Major Salsman says "I am unsure what is wrong with this lady" [see Appendix 19]?

What else does Canadian Forces Shilo Base Surgeon Major Salsman say in his letter [see Appendix 19]?

Salsman goes on to state, "During the stretch of numerous visits she even went to the local Emergency Department. No diagnosis was found then either"?

Is that entirely accurate Salsman?

I think not!

First, Canadian Forces members do not check themselves into the local Emergency Hospital –they do not go off base without permission.

Secondly, in this particular case, it was Salsman's own base medical unit that transported her to the Emergency Hospital.

And, as to that 'unknown' diagnosis Salsman refers to, how about this finding?

This young Canadian Forces female member was taken from her BMQ course by Salsman's own medical unit to the local hospital [Brandon Regional Health Centre] where this young Canadian Forces female member was admitted to Brandon Regional Health Centre on 13 July, 2006 with an infected toe because of the grossly oversized boots she had been issued by my 748 Comm unit with the "area around blister reddened … pus" [see Appendix 13].

And, as to that 'unknown' diagnosis Salsman refers to in his letter dated 17 July, 2006 [see Appendix 19], how about this finding?

As recorded in Salsman's own medical unit at Shilo on 14 July, 2006 it indicated that this young Canadian Forces female member had been "in emergency last night" and the cause is clearly indicated in Salsman's own medical unit's records, a "blister infected right foot" [see Appendix 14].

And finally, as to that 'unknown' diagnosis Salsman refers to in his letter dated 17 July, 2006 [see Appendix 19], how about this finding?

This young Canadian Forces female member was prescribed an antibiotic on 14 July, 2006 for her infected foot by Salsman's own BASE MEDICAL CLINIC [see Appendix 15]?

This guy's a medical doctor?

As Salsman wrote in his apparent "cover-up" letter dated 17 July, 2006, "she even went to the local Emergency Department. No diagnosis was found then either"?

One has to ask?

Any ethics there?

Just look at the facts to apparently indicate no?

This young Canadian Forces female member was taken from her BMQ course by Salsman's own medical unit to the local hospital [Brandon Regional Health Centre] where this young Canadian Forces female member was admitted to Brandon Regional Health Centre on 13 July, 2006 with an infected toe because of the grossly oversized boots she had been issued by my 748 Comm unit with the "area around blister reddened ... pus" [see Appendix 13].

That seems to be a "diagnosis", doesn't it Salsman?

It seems to indicate your comment about an 'unknown' diagnosis in your letter dated 17 July, 2006 [see Appendix 19] is simply a fabrication ["lie"], doesn't it Salsman?

As also recorded in Salsman's own medical unit at Shilo on 14 July, 2006 it indicated that this young Canadian Forces female member had been "in emergency last night" and the cause is clearly indicated in Salsman's own medical unit's records, a "blister infected right foot" [see Appendix 14].

That seems to be a "diagnosis", doesn't it Salsman?

Again, it seems to indicate your comment about an 'unknown' diagnosis in your letter dated 17 July, 2006 [see Appendix 19] is simply a fabrication ["lie"], doesn't it Salsman?

This young Canadian Forces female member was prescribed an antibiotic on 14 July, 2006 for her infected foot by Salsman's own BASE MEDICAL CLINIC [see Appendix 15]?

That seems to be a "diagnosis", doesn't it Salsman?

Once again, it seems to indicate your comment about an 'unknown' diagnosis in your letter dated 17 July, 2006 [see Appendix 19] is simply a fabrication ["lie"], doesn't it Salsman?

What do you think?

Chapter 8

Let's have one last look at Canadian Forces Shilo Base Surgeon Major Salsman's letter to see what other lies it contains?

Let's look at that apparent "cover-up" letter dated 17 July, 2006 written by that Canadian Forces Shilo Base Surgeon Major Salsman one final time [see Appendix 19]?

In it, Canadian Forces Shilo Base Surgeon Major Salsman says "I am unsure what is wrong with this lady" [see Appendix 19]?

What else does Canadian Forces Shilo Base Surgeon Major Salsman say in his letter dated 17 July, 2006 [see Appendix 19]?

Salsman goes on to state: "Once weekend sick parade started she came to that as well … she called the duty medical team to report nefarious symptoms. She was seen again … and still all … were negative"?

Ah, let's get the times down properly and we'll see that Salsman's additional comments are also apparently a 'crock of b.s.'?

Well let's see Salsman, this young Canadian Forces female member was taken from her Shilo BMQ course by Salsman's medical unit to Brandon Regional Health Centre where she was admitted on 13 July, 2006 with an infected toe because of the grossly oversized boots she had been issued by my 748 Comm unit "area around blister reddened … pus" [see Appendix 13].

The 13th of July, 2006 was apparently a Thursday?

This young Canadian Forces female member spent the night at the Emergency.

Hence, she was returned to the Canadian Forces Base at Shilo, Manitoba, Canada on 14 July, 2006 which appears to be a Friday?

At Salsman's own Shilo medical unit, it is recorded on that same Friday [14 July, 2006] that this young Canadian Forces female member had been "in emergency last night" referring to her "blister infected right foot" [see Appendix 14]?

Finally, on that same day in Salsman's own Shilo medical unit this young Canadian Forces female member was prescribed an antibiotic on

14 July, 2006 for her infected foot by Salsman's own BASE MEDICAL CLINIC [see Appendix 15]?

Gee Salsman, this young Canadian Forces female member had "nefarious symptoms" did she?

Hey "Einsten", don't you remember she had an infected foot from the grossly oversized combat boots you actually referred to yourself?

As cited in your medical unit at Shilo Manitoba base camp on 05 July, 2006 "friction marks, hot spots and blisters caused by grossly oversized combat boots" -- Signed by Canadian Forces Shilo Base Surgeon Major Salsman [see Appendix 8].

Maybe too, you forgot your own recommendation on 14 July, 2006 when you saw her that this young Canadian Forces female member should be medically RTU'd to her unit [see Appendix 18, as well as Appendices 16 & 17].

Again, can anyone spell fabrication ["lie"]?

The proof is apparently in the pudding?

As Salsman clearly states in his 17 July, 2006 letter, "she called the duty medical team to report nefarious symptoms. She was seen again … and still all … were negative"?

Hmmm?

As to those 'nefarious symptoms' Salsman refers to in his letter dated 17 July, 2006 [see Appendix 19], how about this finding?

This young Canadian Forces female member was taken from her Shilo BMQ course by Salsman's medical unit to Brandon Regional Health Centre where she was admitted on 13 July, 2006 with an infected toe because of the grossly oversized boots she had been issued by my 748 Comm unit with a recording of "area around blister reddened … pus" in the hospital records [see Appendix 13].

As to those 'nefarious symptoms' Salsman refers to in his letter dated 17 July, 2006 [see Appendix 19], how about this finding?

At Salsman's own Shilo medical unit, it is recorded on 14 July, 2006 that this young Canadian Forces female member had been "in emergency last night" referring to her "blister infected right foot" [see Appendix 14]?

36

Once again, as to those 'nefarious symptoms' Salsman refers to in his letter dated 17 July, 2006 [see Appendix 19], how about this finding?

On that same day in Salsman's own Shilo medical unit this young Canadian Forces female member was prescribed an antibiotic on 14 July, 2006 for her infected foot by Salsman's own BASE MEDICAL CLINIC [see Appendix 15]?

Ah, what's that word again?

Can anyone spell fabrication ["lie"]?

Chapter 9

Apparently don't count on any sort of fair play by Captain D.R. Bowhey at the Nanaimo 748 Comm Unit?

And would her 748 Comm Unit give this young Canadian Forces female member another chance?

No way!

After all, they would have to admit they did not follow procedure when they issued her the "clown sized" boots she was straddled with at "boot camp" [BMQ] as cited in Appendix 7.

As noted earlier, even Canada's General W.Z. Natynczyk on page 3 of his letter dated 29 January, 2010 confirmed that "I find that the boot fitting procedures set out in the supply manual were not followed by supply personnel at 748 Comm Sqn, Nanaimo" [See Appendix 23].

Oh, we can't do that – admit we were wrong?

Never!

So what does the Officer in charge of the Nanaimo 748 Comm Unit do?

Captain D.R. Bowhey gets rid of this young Canadian Forces female member.

This young Canadian Forces female member obtained a complete diagnosis of her suggested plantar fasciitis [originally mentioned on 5 July, 2006 by Canadian Forces Shilo Base Surgeon Major Salsman, see Appendix 9].

As cited, in Dr. Pistone's letter dated 22 February, 2007 it substantiated that this young Canadian Forces female member suffers Bilateral Pes Planus & Posterior tibial dysfunction level 1 [see Appendix 21] which could be remedied by a simple orthotic [see Appendix 22].

Even General W.Z. Natynczyk on page 3 of his letter dated 29 January, 2010 confirms that this young Canadian Forces female member's Plantar Fasciitis [pes planus] is congenital "your foot condition is congenital" [see Appendix 23].

Even the basic studies would confirm military activity aggravates plantar fasciitis.

As cited:

"Most of the injuries to both women and men engaged in military BT are overuse injuries (e.g., achilles tendinitis, patellar-femoral syndrome, plantar fasciitis, and stress fractures)."[1]

And again:

"The overall incidence of plantar fasciitis in the military population was 10.55 per 1,000 person-years."[2]

"Female subjects, when compared with male subjects, had a significantly increased incidence rate ratio for plantar fasciitis of 1.95 (95% CI 1.93-1.98)."[3]

Surely, the Canadian Forces wouldn't let this injustice pursue?

What to do?

Surely an internal grievance against being released from her 748 Comm Unit due to being issued "grossly oversized combat boots" [see Appendix 8] especially as this young female Canadian Forces member suffered from plantar fasciitis would correct the problem?

Guess again?

Footnotes

1. Exercise-Related Injuries Among Women: Strategies for Prevention from Civilian and Military Studies, National Center for Injury Prevention and Control
March 31, 2000 / 49(RR02);13-33

2 – 3. The epidemiology of plantar fasciitis, April 2010.

Chapter 10

What a colossal waste of time complaining to General W.Z. Natynczyk of the Canadian Forces about discrimination!

As advertised:

"Created ten years ago under the National Defense Act, the Board is a federal body with quasi-judicial functions that is independent of the Department of National Defense and the Canadian Forces; it reviews the military grievances referred to it and provides impartial findings and recommendations to the Chief of the Defense Staff and the grievor."[1]

Let's get this straight.

The Grievance Board is a federal body with quasi-judicial functions that is independent of the Department of National Defense and the Canadian Forces, yet it issues it's findings to the Chief of the Defense Staff for final disposition regarding a Canadian Force member's grievance?

Hello, hello – anyone home?

The Chief of the Defense Staff is actually a Canadian Forces / Department of National Defense general?

How impartial is a Canadian Forces / Department of National Defense general going to be with respect to a Canadian Force member's grievance?

Apparently, they aren't?

In this young Canadian Forces female member's case, the Canadian Forces / Department of National Defense general, as you will see, is General W.Z. Natynczyk.

When it comes to Canadian Government "impartiality", it's apparently all 'smoke and mirrors' – it apparently doesn't exist?

Let's see if you agree with this statement after you read about this young Canadian Forces female member's grievance to this so-called "impartial" board?

What you may find is that this so-called "impartial" process is in name only, and in this young Canadian Forces female member's case, it may be quite clear that this board ignored all of her submissions and sided with the apparent fabrication(s) ["lies"] already described in previous chapters and others to be made known below.

As also advertised, this so called impartial grievance process is to be a relatively quick process?

"The Lamer Report recommended that grievances should be answered within 12 months of receipt by the CDS. The Board agrees that this is reasonable and works towards this deadline."[2]

That's apparently also a crock of the proverbial "b.s."?

Let's see now, this young Canadian Forces female member put in her grievance in 2006 and she doesn't get final word until 4 years later in 2010?

Yep, that's pretty darn quick, isn't it?

Talk about dragging one's feet in hopes that the young Canadian Forces female member would loose interest?

Footnotes

1. Message from the Chairperson Bruno Hamel

2. The Lamer Report

Chapter 11

Grievance seems straight forward until General W.Z. Natynczyk gets his hands on it!

Well, let's see what this Canadian Forces "impartial" grievance board did for this young Canadian Forces female member?

The guy writing the final grievance report was General W.Z. Natynczyk.

All indications were he was a good guy?

"Lieutenant-General Walter J. Natynczyk brings strong leadership and unparalleled experience to his new position," Prime Minister Stephen Harper said in a statement Friday. [1]

As also cited, Defense Minister Peter MacKay and Natynczyk spoke to reporters in the House of Commons foyer following the announcement:

"We have great confidence, clearly, in his capability, in his approach to military and this is a very good-news story for Canada," said MacKay. [2]

He was so well liked by his troops who apparently called him "Uncle Walt":

Natynczyk, who is affectionately known among the troops as "Uncle Walt," told reporters he was honoured to be selected as the new CDS. "I'm looking forward to providing the leadership to the men and women of the Canadian Forces. [3]

In fact, as cited in General W.Z. Natynczyk letter dated 29 January, 2010 [see Appendix 23], it does list some positive statements to support this young Canadian Forces female member in her grievance:

Specifically, Quote #1 - page 3: General W.Z. Natynczyk in his letter dated 29 January, 2010 confirms that this young Canadian Forces female member's Plantar Fasciitis [pes planus] is congenital "your foot condition is congenital" [see Appendix 23].

Specifically, Quote #2 - page 4: General W.Z. Natynczyk in his letter dated 29 January, 2010 confirms that because this young Canadian Forces female member had a congenital condition of Plantar Fasciitis she was qualified for orthopaedic footwear according to Canadian Forces Supply Manual "Veteran Affairs Canada defines pes planus, the genetic condition from which you suffer, as a deformed foot. As such, you qualified to be fitted with orthopaedic footwear" [see Appendix 23].

Specifically, Quote #3 - page 3: General W.Z. Natynczyk in his letter dated 29 January, 2010 confirms that because this young Canadian Forces female member had a congenital condition of Plantar Fasciitis she was qualified for orthopaedic footwear according to Canadian Forces Supply Manual and that, as stated in the Canadian Forces Supply Manual that if improper footwear is given (to a soldier recruit) "improper fitted footwear affects the general well being of an individual, often to such an extent as to impair health, morale and efficiency. It is, therefore, of the utmost importance that individuals wear footwear for which they have been measured and properly fitted" [see Appendix 23].

Specifically, Quote #4 - page 3: General W.Z. Natynczyk in his letter dated 29 January, 2010 confirms that "I find that the boot fitting procedures set out in the supply manual were not followed by supply personnel at 748 Comm Sqn, Nanaimo" with regard to this young Canadian Forces female member [see Appendix 23].

Specifically, Quote #5 - page 4: General W.Z. Natynczyk in his letter dated 29 January, 2010 confirms that it was Maj. Salsman who diagnosed the need for special boots for this young Canadian Forces female member due to her Plantar Fasciitis [pes planus] "I find the earliest opportunity at which you could have been assessed as requiring orthopaedic footwear was upon examination by Maj. Salsman" [see Appendix 23].

Well that seems clear enough?

Doesn't it?

It's obvious this young Canadian Forces female member should be issued her special boots to accommodate her Plantar Fasciitis [pes planus] and be given a second chance to do the BMQ course, which she couldn't complete because of the grossly oversized combat boots she was issued by her 748 Comm unit?

That seems fair doesn't it?

As recorded in the medical unit at Shilo Manitoba base camp on 05 July, 2006 "friction marks, hot spots and blisters caused by grossly oversized combat boots" -- Signed by Canadian Forces Shilo Base Surgeon Major Salsman [see Appendix 8].

Guess again?

From there, it's all down hill for this young Canadian Forces female member due to apparent continuing fabrication(s) ["lies"]?

Footnotes

1 - 3. 'Gentleman general' appointed to lead military
CTV.ca News Staff
Date: Fri. Jun. 6 2008 8:42 PM ET

Chapter 12

Is this a "lie" General W.Z. Natynczyk?

Let's look at that stuff again:

As cited in General W.Z. Natynczyk letter dated 29 January, 2010 [see Appendix 23], it does list some positive statements to support this young Canadian Forces female member in her grievance:

Specifically, Quote #1 - page 3: General W.Z. Natynczyk in his letter dated 29 January, 2010 confirms that this young Canadian Forces female member's Plantar Fasciitis [pes planus] is congenital "your foot condition is congenital" [see Appendix 23].

Specifically, Quote #2 - page 4: General W.Z. Natynczyk in his letter dated 29 January, 2010 confirms that because this young Canadian Forces female member had a congenital condition of Plantar Fasciitis she was qualified for orthopaedic footwear according to Canadian Forces Supply Manual "Veteran Affairs Canada defines pes planus, the genetic condition from which you suffer, as a deformed foot. As such, you qualified to be fitted with orthopaedic footwear" [see Appendix 23].

Specifically, Quote #3 - page 3: General W.Z. Natynczyk in his letter dated 29 January, 2010 confirms that because this young Canadian Forces female member had a congenital condition of Plantar Fasciitis she was qualified for orthopaedic footwear according to Canadian Forces Supply Manual and that, as stated in the Canadian Forces Supply Manual that if improper footwear is given (to a soldier recruit) "improper fitted footwear affects the general well being of an individual, often to such an extent as to impair health, morale and efficiency. It is, therefore, of the utmost importance that individuals wear footwear for which they have been measured and properly fitted" [see Appendix 23].

Specifically, Quote #4 - page 3: General W.Z. Natynczyk in his letter dated 29 January, 2010 confirms that "I find that the boot fitting procedures set out in the supply manual were not followed by supply personnel at 748 Comm Sqn, Nanaimo" with regard to this young Canadian Forces female member [see Appendix 23].

Specifically, Quote #5 - page 4: General W.Z. Natynczyk in his letter dated 29 January, 2010 confirms that it was Maj. Salsman who diagnosed the need for special boots for this young Canadian Forces female member due to her Plantar Fasciitis [pes planus] "I find the earliest opportunity at which you could have been assessed as requiring orthopaedic footwear was upon examination by Maj. Salsman" [see Appendix 23].

Great, where are the special boots?

However, these special boots were <u>never</u> given to this young Canadian Forces female member?

Ah, the apparent fabrication(s) ["lies"] continue?

Specifically, Quote #6 - page 4: General W.Z. Natynczyk in his letter dated 29 January, 2010 confirms that it was Maj. Salsman who diagnosed the need for special boots for this young Canadian Forces female member due to her Plantar Fasciitis [pes planus] "and that his recommendation was accepted and acted upon immediately".

Hey, wait a minute "Uncle Walt"?

This young Canadian Forces female member <u>never</u> did receive these special boots?

A fabrication ["lie"]?

What's wrong "Uncle Walt"?

No time for this young Canadian Forces female member?

Oh, "Uncle Walt", don't tell me you can't support this young Canadian Forces female member's grievance at any cost?

Don't tell me "Uncle Walt" that this is the ultimate task of the "impartial" grievance process?

Support the Canadian Forces at any cost to this 'little gal'?

Chapter 13

The nice thing about liars, they commit more and more lies trying to protect themselves?

As mentioned, the nice thing about liars, they commit more and more lies trying to protect themselves?

Eventually the lies become obvious?

Ask any good police detective.

That's how cases are solved.

Sort of reminds the author of this case.

Incredibly, in another high profile case, another senior RCMP officer lied again and again.

The so-called RCMP expert witness, classed an expert witness on blood-pattern analyses, was "accused of perjury and exposed in B.C. Supreme Court as the author of a flawed forensic report that got basic biology wrong."[1]

Who was this RCMP Officer?

"Staff Sgt. Ross Spenard's credibility was shredded during the recent second-degree murder trial of Charlie Rae Lincoln, an aboriginal woman convicted of stabbing to death her own two-year-old. He acknowledged misleading the court and failing to send a letter to the Crown in the case revealing the concerns about the report and his errors."[2]

RCMP Spenard thought he covered his tracks by shredding documents.

He was wrong.

As noted, "armed with a copy of documents that Spenard thought were destroyed, defense lawyer Matthew Nathanson forced him to make a series of devastating admissions."[3]

The document was riddled with so many DNA misinterpretations and errors that the top experts in the field were flown in from Edmonton and Halifax to correct it. Some conclusions were "not scientifically sound," they said.[4]

"You were not being truthful, right?" the lawyer said, confronting the Mountie with a transcript of his earlier testimony.[5]

"Yes, I agree" Spenard admitted.[6]

"You will recall the Staff Sgt. Spenard gave some evidence of blood found in... [a] house at different places," the justice said before sending the jurors to deliberate. "You have heard the Crown totally ignore his evidence, and I suggest to you that you do ignore his evidence completely.[8]

"Staff. Sgt. Spenard is the perfect example of a person who clearly lied under oath, and violated his oath to tell the truth, and he even agreed to this. That conclusion is so clear and convincing, and so serious, that I suggest you should consider his evidence to be completely tainted, and without any value whatsoever."[9]

Again, Holey smokes?

If members of the Royal Canadian Mounted Police apparently lie[10], it would seem that some other employees of the Canadian Government are apparently equally able to lie too?

Could this be true?

Would this include some members of the Canadian Forces?

The comment on page 4 of General W.Z. Natynczyk letter dated 29 January, 2010 clearly indicates it was Maj. Salsman who diagnosed the need for special boots for this young Canadian Forces female member due to her Plantar Fasciitis [pes planus] "and that his recommendation was accepted and acted upon immediately".

As cited, this young Canadian Forces female member was never issued these special boots?

Footnotes

1 - 9. Caught in a web of documents he thought had been destroyed: Blood-splatter expert admits to misleading court and failing to send a letter to the Crown revealing concerns about the forensic report.
Ian Mulgrew, Vancouver Sun, June 29, 2009.
[see Appendix 11]

10. Also reference to: The Very Thin Red Line: This police force is

"horribly broken". Amazon.com

Chapter 14

Let's look at General W.Z. Natynczyk's lie again!

Now that the shock has worn off, let's have another look at General W.Z. Natynczyk's statement again.

Specifically, Quote #6 - page 4: General W.Z. Natynczyk in his letter dated 29 January, 2010 confirms that it was Maj. Salsman who diagnosed the need for special boots for this young Canadian Forces female member due to her Plantar Fasciitis [pes planus] "and that his recommendation was accepted and acted upon immediately".

Again, hey wait a minute "Uncle Walt"?

This young Canadian Forces female member never did receive these special boots?

That's like some emergency doctor ordering an immediate operation for a patient, but the patient never receives that operation because the patient is forgotten in the hallway and never makes it to the operating room?

The patient died!

It's the same for this young Canadian Forces female member, on 10 July, 2006 Canadian Forces Shilo Base Surgeon Major Salsman ordered special boots for this young Canadian Forces female member so she could perform her military duties [see Appendix 12].

Just like the emergency doctor ordering an immediate operation?

However, just like the patient who never received the immediate operation, this young Canadian Forces female member never did receive these special boots?

She too 'died' on the BMQ course.

Without these essential special boots, she was unable to complete the majority of the BMQ course.

As cited previously, due to the severe medical problems caused by the "grossly oversized boots" issued by her 748 Comm Unit [see Appendix 8], this young Canadian Forces female member was unable to complete the majority of the BMQ course [see Appendix 20].

She was unable to complete "Survive under NBC conditions" nor the "Field training" nor the "Drills" and neither the "Service rifle" [see Appendix 20].

So, "Uncle Walt", what kind of illogic are you using when you say "and that his recommendation was accepted and acted upon immediately" when this young Canadian Forces female member never did receive those special combat boots so she could perform her military duties?

Your statement "Uncle Walt" doesn't make any sense, unless [God forbid] your primary goal was to not support this young Canadian Forces female member's grievance at any cost?

Support the Canadian Forces at any cost to the detriment of this 'little gal'?

Ah, "Uncle Walt", tell me it isn't so?

After all, she's only one little lone individual against the might of the Department of National Defense / Canadian Forces?

What can she do, if you screw with her?

Oh, "Uncle Walt", tell me it isn't so?

Chapter 15

Is this another lie by General W.Z. Natynczyk?

Let's look again at General W.Z. Natynczyk letter dated 29 January, 2010 [see Appendix 23].

Incredibly, "Uncle Walt" in his letter dated 29 January, 2010 now tries to white wash the obvious oversized boots by saying that they were a perfect fit as per Quote #7 - Page 3 "the shortest standard sized combat boot that will accommodate your width corresponds exactly to the boot you were issued" [see Appendix 23 for this guy's "analysis" of the combat boots cited on page 3 of his 29 January, 2010 letter and as issued to this young Canadian Forces female member].

What?

A Canadian Forces general says the "clown sized" boots [see Appendix 7] were an exact fit?

Specifically, General W.Z. Natynczyk says his letter dated 29 January, 2010 as per Quote #7 - Page 3 "the shortest standard sized combat boot that will accommodate your width corresponds exactly to the boot you were issued" [see Appendix 23].

Do you agree with "Uncle Walt"?

The "Clown Sized" boots issued to this young Canadian Forces female member was an exact fit [see Appendix 7]?

One has to ask, what is "Uncle Walt" on?

Just look at the "grossly oversized combat boots" and the size of this young Canadian Forces female member's feet [see Appendix 7] and see if you agree with "Uncle Walt's" conclusion that these boots are an exact fit for this young Canadian Forces female member?

Even that Salsman recognized the boots were far too big for this young Canadian Forces female member: As recorded in the medical unit at Shilo Manitoba base camp on 05 July, 2006 "friction marks, hot spots and blisters caused by grossly oversized combat boots" -- Signed by Canadian Forces Shilo Base Surgeon Major Salsman [see Appendix 8].

Again, what's wrong "Uncle Walt"?

No time for this young Canadian Forces female member?

Ah yes, I forgot, maybe your hidden mandate was not to support this young Canadian Forces female member's grievance at any cost?

Isn't that the ultimate task of the "impartial" grievance process?

Support the Canadian Forces at any cost to the detriment of this 'little gal'?

Chapter 16

Is this yet another lie by General W.Z. Natynczyk?

Let's look once again at General W.Z. Natynczyk letter dated 29 January, 2010 [see Appendix 23].

Incredibly, "Uncle Walt" in his letter dated 29 January, 2010 now tries to white wash the blisters and foot infection suffered by this young Canadian Forces female member "caused by grossly oversized combat boots" when Natynczyk says on page 3 of his letter "I further find that the temporary foot blisters were corrected with mild pain reliever and antibiotics."

What?

Is "Uncle Walt" 'out to lunch'?

Did "Uncle Walt" forget or just simply ignore this information?

On 05 July, 2006 the medical unit at Shilo Manitoba base camp recorded "blisters and hot spots" on left and right foot -- Signed by Canadian Forces Shilo Base Surgeon Major Salsman [See Appendix 8].

Also recorded in the medical unit at Shilo Manitoba base camp on 05 July, 2006 "on left foot there is a 1" long friction mark on the posterior aspect of the foot slightly proximal from the 'calcaneus(?)'. There is also a blister on the plantar aspect of the foot located on the heel. It appears to be relatively deep. On the right foot there is a similar friction mark as described on the left foot. There are hot spots located on the bottom of both heels" -- Signed by Canadian Forces Shilo Base Surgeon Major Salsman [see Appendix 8].

As also recorded in the medical unit at Shilo Manitoba base camp on 05 July, 2006 "friction marks, hot spots and blisters caused by grossly oversized combat boots" -- Signed by Canadian Forces Shilo Base Surgeon Major Salsman [see Appendix 8].

As also recorded in the medical unit at Shilo Manitoba base camp on 05 July, 2006 "enquire about new boots, should be fitted with orthotics, and dressed friction marks, dressed with 'hypafix(?)' and 'mepore(?)' -- Signed by Canadian Forces Shilo Base Surgeon Major Salsman [see Appendix 8].

It was also at this time that Canadian Forces Shilo Base Surgeon Major Salsman gave this young Canadian Forces female member a pamphlet on plantar fasciitis [see Appendix 9].

Also recorded   in the medical unit at Shilo Manitoba base camp on 05 July, 2006 specific instructions that this young Canadian Forces female member should not drill, not march, not run, and no ruck or webbing marches [see Appendix 10].

Good God, how on earth could this young Canadian Forces female member pass the BMQ if her feet were so bad because of the idiotic "grossly oversized combat boots" fitted her by her 748 Communications Unit?

Again, as recorded on 07 July, 2006 specific instructions for this young Canadian Forces female member indicated she should not drill, not march, and no ruck or webbing marches and this time no prolonged standing for more than 20 minutes [see Appendix 11].

Good God, again how on earth could this young Canadian Forces female member pass the BMQ if she couldn't stand for more than 20 minutes – any parade activity sometimes takes hours of standing?

The end result, this young Canadian Forces female member was taken from her BMQ course and admitted to Brandon Regional Health Centre on 13 July, 2006 with an infected toe because of the grossly oversized boots she had been issued by my 748 Comm unit "area around blister reddened ... pus" [see Appendix 13].

Finally, as recorded in the medical unit at Shilo Manitoba base camp on 14 July, 2006 it indicated that this young Canadian Forces female member had been "in emergency last night" and then referred to "blister infected right foot" [see Appendix 14].

This young Canadian Forces female member was prescribed an antibiotic for her infected foot [see Appendix 15].

Has "Uncle Walt" ever marched around with infected feet?

Why don't you try it "Uncle Walt" and then write your 'idiotic' comment, "I further find that the temporary foot blisters were corrected with mild pain reliever and antibiotics" [see Appendix 23].

The usual time frame for the antibiotic [see Appendix 15] prescribed to this young female Canadian Forces member is 10 days, for example, Apo-Cephalex 250 mg 4x/day for 10 days?

Again, what's wrong "Uncle Walt"?

Still no time for this young Canadian Forces female member?

Ah yes, the apparent hidden mandate of this "impartial" board, can't support this young Canadian Forces female member's grievance at any cost?

The buz word is, support the Canadian Forces at any cost to the 'little gal', isn't it?

Tell me it isn't so, "Uncle Walt"?

"Uncle Walt"?

"Uncle Walt"?

Are you there?

I guess not?

Why else would "Uncle Walt" come to the equally 'idiotic' conclusion, "I am satisfied that you [this young Canadian Forces female member] have been treated appropriately" as cited in his letter dated 29 January, 2010 [see Appendix 23]?

What?

Chapter 17

When the 'shite' hits the fan - – the rats will apparently scurry to cover their 'arses'!

Let's go back and have another look at those "grossly oversized combat boots" [see Appendix 7 and Appendix 8].

If you will excuse the expression, when the 'shite' hits the fan – the rats will apparently scurry to cover their 'arses'!

As cited, the photos of this young Canadian Forces female member's grossly oversized combat boots [see Appendix 7] "originated by a Sergeant at the Shilo Health Services Unit on 5 July 2006 and depict the griever's feet with bandaged heels, next to the combat boots that extend several inches beyond her toes. The e-mail photos were sent under the heading "oversized boots" up the Chain of Command to the Comm Res School and to the griever's unit" [From Canadian Forces Grievance Board file # 2007-076, see Appendix 24].

Oh, oh – the jig is up?

Remember that General W.Z. Natynczyk on page 3 of his letter dated 29 January, 2010 confirmed that "I find that the boot fitting procedures set out in the supply manual were not followed by supply personnel at 748 Comm Sqn, Nanaimo" with regard to this young Canadian Forces female member [see Appendix 23].

What to do, let's respond with this.

"In response to these emails, the Ops WO explained the procedures followed by the unit to issue the grievor's combat boots. Contrary to the grievor's assertion that she complained to personnel at the unit about her boots, the Ops WO indicated that the grievor had never indicated there was a problem" [From Canadian Forces Grievance Board file # 2007-076, see Appendix 25].

Another fabrication ["lie"]?

Appears to be?

Especially since General W.Z. Natynczyk on page 3 of his letter dated 29 January, 2010 confirmed that "I find that the boot fitting procedures set out in the supply manual were not followed by supply personnel at 748 Comm Sqn, Nanaimo" with regard to this young Canadian Forces female member [see Appendix 23].

In fact, no sooner was this young Canadian Forces female member in the Nanaimo 748 Communications Unit, she noticed her boots didn't fit [see Appendix 7].

After all, this young Canadian Forces female member had spend 4 years in Air Cadets with proper fitting combat boots and she well knew a proper fitting combat boot from the idiotic "Clown Sized" combat boot this Nanaimo Comm Unit was trying to pawn off on her [see Appendix 7].

Again, remember that General W.Z. Natynczyk on page 3 of his letter dated 29 January, 2010 confirmed that "I find that the boot fitting procedures set out in the supply manual were not followed by supply personnel at 748 Comm Sqn, Nanaimo" with regard to this young Canadian Forces female member [see Appendix 23].

In spite of her attempts to correct the problem, she was sent to "boot camp" [Canada's BMQ] with these "clown sized" boots [see Appendix 7].

In fact, since being released from the Canadian Forces, this young Canadian Forces female member has held responsible positions in security with proper fitting combat boots, with simple orthotics to accommodate her plantar fasciitis with no problems whatsoever.

As such, it becomes very obvious, the efforts of the Ops WO was apparently simply a ploy to try to blame the victim [From Canadian Forces Grievance Board file # 2007-076, see Appendix 25]?

Once again, remember that General W.Z. Natynczyk on page 3 of his letter dated 29 January, 2010 confirmed that "I find that the boot fitting procedures set out in the supply manual were not followed by supply personnel at 748 Comm Sqn, Nanaimo" with regard to this young Canadian Forces female member [see Appendix 23].

It's a trick by governments and defense lawyers – blame the victim – detract from the culprit.

For example, in this Government case, "a federal judge in Boston yesterday found that the Justice Department tried to humiliate and embarrass the families of two women who were murdered by longtime FBI informants James "Whitey" Bulger and Stephen "the Rifleman" Flemmi by unfairly blaming the victims for their own deaths during a lengthy civil trial last year over a wrongful death suit brought against the agency.[1]

US District Judge William G. Young ordered the government to pay $5,000 each to the families of Debra Davis and Deborah Hussey, who were slain in the 1980s, for legal fees that resulted from "responding to a meritless defense raised with the sole purpose of embarrassing'' the women's families.[2]

The government had argued that both women and their families were negligent because they had personal relationships with Flemmi that put them at risk.[3]

In a separate ruling yesterday, Young refused to reconsider his earlier finding that the Justice Department must pay hefty legal fees to the mother of another Bulger victim, John McIn tyre of Quincy, for acting in bad faith by deliberately withholding evidence of FBI corruption in a bid to get that case dismissed before it went to trial four years ago.[4]

The government already had been found liable for all three deaths because of the FBI's mishandling of Bulger, who fled in 1995 and remains a fugitive wanted for 19 murders, and Flemmi, who is serving a life sentence for 10 slayings. But Young's rulings condemn the way Justice Department lawyers from Washington defended the civil cases.[5]

"To blame these victims is a little beyond the pale, and I think that's why he sanctioned them,'' said Milton lawyer Paul J. Griffin, who represents the Davis family.[6]

Gosh sakes?

If the FBI can try to blame the victims, why not the Canadian Forces?

In the case of our young Canadian Forces female member, the proof that the Ops WO [see Appendix 25] is apparently full of baloney is in General W.Z. Natynczyk own comment.

As cite on page 3 of General W.Z. Natynczyk's letter dated 29 January, 2010 confirmed that "I find that the boot fitting procedures set out in the supply manual were <u>not</u> followed by supply personnel at 748 Comm Sqn, Nanaimo" [See Appendix 23].

Footnotes

1 – 6. Judge raps US over Bulger civil trial

Says victims, families were unfairly blamed
By Shelley Murphy
Globe Staff, 25 September, 2010

Chapter 18

Y. Couture, Commander, National Defense Headquarters tries to blame the young female soldier – what an "arse"!

You would think that General W.Z. Natynczyk comment would put an end to the Ops WO lame excuse / apparent fabrication ["lie"]?

As cite on page 3 of General W.Z. Natynczyk's letter dated 29 January, 2010 confirmed that "I find that the boot fitting procedures set out in the supply manual were not followed by supply personnel at 748 Comm Sqn, Nanaimo" [See Appendix 23].

Apparently not the Canadian Armed Forces, they'll apparently use any lame excuse / apparent fabrication ["lie"] they can to apparently not support this young Canadian Forces female member's grievance.

Apparently at any cost [fabrication or "lie"]?

As cited, in a letter dated 7 July, 2010 sent to Kathryn Lavery, Early Resolution Advisor, Canadian Human Rights Commission, Suite 1645 Canada Place, 9700 Jasper Avenue, Edmonton, Alberta, Canada T5J 4C3 by Y. Couture, Commander, National Defense Headquarters, this person again uses Ops WO lame excuse / apparent fabrication ["lie"] [see Appendix 26]?

Specifically, on pages 1 & 2, Y. Couture, Commander, National Defense Headquarters again tries to blame the victim [this young Canadian Forces female member] with her final sentence being "the complainant did not choose to exchange kit, nor did she inform anyone that she was still experiencing foot problems" [see Appendix 26].

Hmm, very strange?

Didn't the Ops WO in his rendition of this matter say "He also indicated that he thought the problem had been corrected" [see Appendix 25].

Let's try to get your stories straight?

When the 'shite' hits the fan – the rats will apparently scurry to cover their 'asses'?

One Canadian Forces member [Y. Couture, Commander, National Defense Headquarters] is saying the problem has not been fixed

[Appendix 26] whereas another Canadian Forces member [the Ops WO] is saying the problem had been fixed [Appendix 25]?

Again, let's try to get your stories straight?

Guess what, it doesn't matter what apparent fabrication ["lies"] that the Ops WO [see Appendix 25] or Y. Couture, Commander, National Defense Headquarters [see Appendix 26] may be apparently trying to perpetrate – what matters is General W.Z. Natynczyk concluding comment.

As cite on page 3 of General W.Z. Natynczyk's letter dated 29 January, 2010 confirmed that "I find that the boot fitting procedures set out in the supply manual were not followed by supply personnel at 748 Comm Sqn, Nanaimo" [See Appendix 23].

Incredibly, this Kathryn Lavery of the Canadian Human Rights Commission apparently ignores these facts as later chapters will reveal.

So let's look at that again, after all some members of the Canadian Forces appear to be "a bit dense" when it comes to such matters, "I find that the boot fitting procedures set out in the supply manual were not followed by supply personnel at 748 Comm Sqn, Nanaimo" [See Appendix 23].

That is, the procedures were NOT followed?

Again, as mentioned, the Ops WO's [see Appendix 25] and that of Y. Couture [see Appendix 26] contradictory lame excuses may have washed, except for the fact that this young Canadian Forces female member had spend 4 years in Air Cadets with proper fitting boots and she well knew a proper fitting boot from the idiotic boot this Comm Unit was trying to pawn off on her [see Appendix 7].

In fact, no sooner was this young Canadian Forces female member in the Nanaimo 748 Communications Unit, she noticed her boots didn't fit [see Appendix 7].

In spite of her attempts to correct the problem, she was sent to "boot camp" [Canada's BMQ] with these boots [see Appendix 7].

In fact, since being released from the Canadian Forces, this young Canadian Forces female member has held responsible positions in security with proper fitting combat boots, with simple orthotics to accommodate her plantar fasciitis with no problems whatsoever.

As such, it becomes apparently very obvious, the efforts of the Ops WO [see Appendix 25] and that of Y. Couture [see Appendix 26] was simply an apparent ploy to try to blame the victim?

As mentioned, it's a favorite trick used by governments and defense lawyers – blame the victim – detract from the culprit(s).[1]

Footnotes

1. Judge raps US over Bulger civil trial
Says victims, families were unfairly blamed
By Shelley Murphy
Globe Staff, 25 September, 2010

Chapter 19

As the lies accumulate, it's harder for the liars to keep track of their lies!

Sort of reminds the author of conspirators that lie?

These lies are even harder to keep track of than those of a single person?

Again, just ask any good police detective.

A chink in one conspirator's lie eventually leads to a crumbling of the conspiracy of lies.

For example, in one case, "an RCMP constable who broke a man's jaw on both sides with punches has been found guilty of assault causing bodily, a provincial court judge ruled."[1]

"Evidence at the trial that ended last month indicated that Const. Donovan Tait and his partner were investigating a theft complaint in May 2003 when they confronted Asmeron Yohannes at his North Vancouver home. Tait's defense was that the degree of force used was appropriate because Yohannes spit in the officer's face."[2]

An RCMP fabrication?

Apparently yes?

In her ruling, however, released Tuesday, provincial court Chief Judge Carol Baird Ellan said Tait's story isn't credible and that he arrested Yohannes out of frustration.[3]

The accused partner, Const. Simon Scott, testified that Yohannes spit in Tait's face.[4]

The judge said his testimony "was so rife with discrepancies and contradictions that it would be unreliable."[5]

In fact, possibly the most notorious case of conspirator lies has to do with the vicious tasering to death of 40-year-old Polish immigrant Robert Dziekanski. [6]

Richmond RCMP Sgt. Pierre Lemaitre said officers struggled to subdue the man: 'Even though he had received what they call pulses, two pulses from Taser, he was still out of control.'[7]

"After the event, the Mounties all gave similar statements about how Dziekanski had come at them, yelling and wildly swinging the stapler, and how several officers had to wrestle the man to the ground."[8]

However, a video proved the RCMP officers outright lied!

A witness's video of the event showed none of that happened ... if not for the video, might have got away with whitewashing what the judge called the force's "shameful" conduct in the events that led to an innocent man's death.[9]

Incredibly, "on Dec. 12, 2008, B.C. Criminal Justice branch spokesman Stan Lowe "cleared" the four officers of any wrongdoing and portrayed Dziekanski as a violent and agitated alcoholic whose irrational behavior contributed to his own death."[10]

However, even this Stan Lowe was put in his place when Cisowski had the satisfaction of hearing Thomas Braidwood call the four Mounties "inappropriately aggressive" and "patently unbelievable," while emphasizing Dziekanski did nothing wrong nor in any way caused his own death.[11]

Braidwood called the bystander video by Paul Pritchard of Dziekanski's Tasering death "invaluable" evidence that "couldn't be cross-examined."[12]

"Onlookers were incredulous when RCMP Commissioner William Elliott said Friday he wouldn't be announcing any disciplinary measures for any of the four Mounties for their role in Dziekanski's death."[13]

As noted, "we have seen often-quoted Mountie mouthpiece Cpl. Dale Carr tell the Braidwood inquiry that top RCMP brass made a deliberate decision not to correct misinformation RCMP had given to the media about Dziekanski's death."[14]

In fact, "e-mail suggests four RCMP Officers committed perjury while senior officers sat silent,"[2] specifically suggests Mounties planned to deploy Taser before they arrived at YVR, contrary to their testimony.[15]

As reported, "after months of outrage about the conduct of the four Mounties who responded to Vancouver Airport Oct. 14, 2007, who can believe that at the last minute, a federal lawyer would produce what many would consider a smoking gun -- an e-mail saying the officers decided to use the Taser before confronting the Polish immigrant?"[16]

"If true, the Nov. 5, 2007, e-mail titled "Media strategy -- release of the YVR video," from RCMP Chief Supt. Dick Bent to assistant commissioner Al McIntyre, establishes the four have been lying through their teeth. This critical document suggests the four officers committed perjury and that senior officers sat silent while they did so."[17]

"It's a stunning turn of events," Don Rosenbloom, the lawyer representing the government of Poland at the inquiry.[18]

Rosenbloom said the 11th-hour disclosure "is totally inconsistent with testimony given under oath" and goes to the heart of the issue of police fabrication. During the hearing, he said, "we were alleging [the four Mounties] were fabricating their story."[19]

Incredibly, Commissioner William Elliott's carefully parsed press release was equally unbelievable: "This was simply an oversight. Unfortunately in an exercise of this magnitude, such an oversight can occur."[20]

Elliott a moron, as cited, "no one but a moron overlooks the import of an e-mail like this".[21]

Wow, the RCMP Commissioner, William Elliott, being called a 'moron' in this article.[22]

Once again, wow!

Again, if the Royal Canadian Mounted Police conspire to lie, it would seem that some others working as Canadian Government agents are apparently equally able to lie too?

And one would think that would apparently also includes some members of the Canadian Forces.

After all, didn't the Ops WO in his rendition of this matter say "He also indicated that he thought the problem had been corrected" [see Appendix 25].

Whereas Y. Couture, Commander, National Defense Headquarters in her final sentence stated "the complainant ... was still experiencing foot problems" [see Appendix 26].

As mentioned, 'It's try to get your stories straight?

One Canadian Forces member [Y. Couture, Commander, National Defense Headquarters] is saying the problem has not been fixed [Appendix 26] whereas another Canadian Forces member [the Ops WO] is saying the problem had been fixed [Appendix 25]?

Again, let's try to get your stories straight?

Guess what, it doesn't matter what apparent fabrication ["lies"] that the Ops WO [see Appendix 25] or Y. Couture, Commander, National Defense Headquarters [see Appendix 26] may be apparently trying to perpetrate – what matters is General W.Z. Natynczyk concluding comment.

As cite on page 3 of General W.Z. Natynczyk's letter dated 29 January, 2010 confirmed that "I find that the boot fitting procedures set out in the supply manual were not followed by supply personnel at 748 Comm Sqn, Nanaimo" [See Appendix 23].

Footnotes

1 - 5. RCMP "officer" guilty in North Vancouver assault. Canadian Press. Tuesday, February 15, 2005.

6 - 7. RCMP say deceased man was 40-year-old Polish immigrant Robert Dziekanski. Last Updated: Tuesday, October 16, 2007. CBC News.

8 - 9. Inquiry deservedly hammers RCMP in Dziekanski death. By Paul Schneiderit, The Chronicle Herald, Tue. Jun 22.

10 – 13. 'Still they get no consequences'. By Suzanne Fournier, The Province, June 20, 2010.

14. RCMP admissions in Dziekanski Taser death are troubling. By Damian Inwood, Wed, Apr 22 2009.

15. E-mail Suggests Four RCMP Officers Committed Perjury While Senior Officers Sat Silent. Contributed on Sun, 2009/06/21 - 2:30pm.

Reference also to: Startling New Email Halts Inquiry. By Neal Hall and Lori Culbert; June 20, 2009 - Vancouver Sun.

16 – 17. Damning e-mail suggests the four officers committed perjury and that senior officers sat silent while they did. By Ian Mulgrew; June 20, 2009 - Vancouver Sun.

18 - 19. Startling New Email Halts Inquiry. By Neal Hall and Lori Culbert; June 20, 2009 - Vancouver Sun.

20 - 22. Damning e-mail suggests the four officers committed perjury and that senior officers sat silent while they did. By Ian Mulgrew; June 20, 2009 - Vancouver Sun.

Also reference to: The Very Thin Red Line: This police force is "horribly broken". Amazon.com

Chapter 20

Kathryn Lavery of the Canadian Human Rights Commission accepts lame excuses!

What is most troubling in this matter is that the Canadian Human Rights Commission [agent Kathryn Lavery], as we will see later in this book, apparently accepted these lame excuses against this young female Canadian Forces member in spite of General W.Z. Natynczyk's comment on page 3 of his letter dated 29 January, 2010 confirming that "I find that the boot fitting procedures set out in the supply manual were not followed by supply personnel at 748 Comm Sqn, Nanaimo" [See Appendix 23].

In addition, as will be seen in later chapters in this book, the Canadian Human Rights Commission [agent Kathryn Lavery] also apparently accepted this outright false statement by Y. Couture, Commander, National Defense Headquarters that this young female Canadian Forces member was not issued the corrective boots by her Nanaimo, British Columbia, Canada 748 Comm Unit because she "had already commenced her release proceedings" [see Appendix 27].

In actual fact, this young female Canadian Forces member had been fired [released in spite of her protests] by the commanding officer of her Nanaimo, British Columbia, Canada 748 Comm Unit, that being Captain D.R. Bowhey.

Incredibly, this Kathryn Lavery of the Canadian Human Rights Commission apparently ignores these facts as later chapters will reveal.

In fact this young female Canadian Forces member had the feeling that this Kathryn Lavery of the Canadian Human Rights Commission was biased against her, and even wrote a letter dated 17 July, 2010 expressing such feelings [see Appendix 28].

Chapter 21

The internal grievance process with the Canadian Forces under General W.Z. Natynczyk was nothing but a sham!

Well, what to do?

It was apparent the internal grievance process with the Canadian Forces was nothing but a sham.

In spite of this: Quote #1 - page 3: General W.Z. Natynczyk in his letter dated 29 January, 2010 confirms that this young Canadian Forces female member's Plantar Fasciitis [pes planus] is congenital "your foot condition is congenital" [see Appendix 23].

In spite of this: Quote #2 - page 4: General W.Z. Natynczyk in his letter dated 29 January, 2010 confirms that because this young Canadian Forces female member had a congenital condition of Plantar Fasciitis she was qualified for orthopaedic footwear according to Canadian Forces Supply Manual "Veteran Affairs Canada defines pes planus, the genetic condition from which you suffer, as a deformed foot. As such, you qualified to be fitted with orthopaedic footwear" [see Appendix 23].

In spite of this: Quote #3 - page 3: General W.Z. Natynczyk in his letter dated 29 January, 2010 confirms that because this young Canadian Forces female member had a congenital condition of Plantar Fasciitis she was qualified for orthopaedic footwear according to Canadian Forces Supply Manual and that, as stated in the Canadian Forces Supply Manual that if improper footwear is given (to a soldier recruit) "improper fitted footwear affects the general well being of an individual, often to such an extent as to impair health, morale and efficiency. It is, therefore, of the utmost importance that individuals wear footwear for which they have been measured and properly fitted" [see Appendix 23].

In spite of this: Quote #4 - page 3: General W.Z. Natynczyk in his letter dated 29 January, 2010 confirms that "I find that the boot fitting procedures set out in the supply manual were not followed by supply personnel at 748 Comm Sqn, Nanaimo" with regard to this young Canadian Forces female member [see Appendix 23].

In spite of this: Quote #5 - page 4: General W.Z. Natynczyk in his letter dated 29 January, 2010 confirms that it was Maj. Salsman who diagnosed the need for special boots for this young Canadian Forces female member due to her Plantar Fasciitis [pes planus] "I find the earliest opportunity at which you could have been assessed as requiring orthopaedic footwear was upon examination by Maj. Salsman" [see Appendix 23].

In spite of this: On 10 July, 2006 Canadian Forces Shilo Base Surgeon Major Salsman ordered special boots for this young Canadian Forces female member so she could perform her military duties [see Appendix 12].

In spite of this: On 05 July, 2006 the medical unit at Shilo Manitoba base camp recorded "blisters and hot spots" on left and right foot -- Signed by Canadian Forces Shilo Base Surgeon Major Salsman [See Appendix 8].

In spite of this: Also recorded in the medical unit at Shilo Manitoba base camp on 05 July, 2006 "on left foot there is a 1" long friction mark on the posterior aspect of the foot slightly proximal from the 'calcaneus(?)'. There is also a blister on the plantar aspect of the foot located on the heel. It appears to be relatively deep. On the right foot there is a similar friction mark as described on the left foot. There are hot spots located on the bottom of both heels" -- Signed by Canadian Forces Shilo Base Surgeon Major Salsman [see Appendix 8].

In spite of this: As also recorded in the medical unit at Shilo Manitoba base camp on 05 July, 2006 "friction marks, hot spots and blisters <u>caused by grossly oversized combat boots</u>" -- Signed by Canadian Forces Shilo Base Surgeon Major Salsman [see Appendix 8].

In spite of this: As also recorded in the medical unit at Shilo Manitoba base camp on 05 July, 2006 "enquire about new boots, should be fitted with orthotics, and dressed friction marks, dressed with 'hypafix(?)' and 'mepore(?)' -- Signed by Canadian Forces Shilo Base Surgeon Major Salsman [see Appendix 8].

In spite of this: It was also at this time that Canadian Forces Shilo Base Surgeon Major Salsman gave this young Canadian Forces female member a pamphlet on plantar fasciitis [see Appendix 9].

In spite of this: Also recorded in the medical unit at Shilo Manitoba base camp on 05 July, 2006 specific instructions that this young Canadian Forces female member should <u>not</u> drill, <u>not</u> march, <u>not</u> run, and <u>no</u> ruck or webbing marches [see Appendix 10].

In spite of this: Again, as recorded on 07 July, 2006 specific instructions for this young Canadian Forces female member indicated she should <u>not</u> drill, <u>not</u> march, and <u>no</u> ruck or webbing marches and this time <u>no</u> prolonged standing for more than 20 minutes [see Appendix 11].

In spite of this: The end result, this young Canadian Forces female member was taken from her BMQ course and admitted to Brandon Regional Health Centre on 13 July, 2006 with an infected toe because of the grossly oversized boots she had been issued by my 748 Comm unit "area around blister reddened … pus" [see Appendix 13].

In spite of this: As recorded in the medical unit at Shilo Manitoba base camp on 14 July, 2006 it indicated that this young Canadian Forces female member had been "in emergency last night" and then referred to "blister infected right foot" [see Appendix 14].

In spite of this: This young Canadian Forces female member was prescribed an antibiotic for her infected foot [see Appendix 15].

Yet, old "Uncle Walt" [General W.Z. Natynczyk] nevertheless concluded "I am satisfied that you [this young Canadian Forces female member] have been treated appropriately" [see Appendix 23].

In addition, old "Uncle Walt" [General W.Z. Natynczyk] added apparent fabrication with: Quote #6 - page 4: General W.Z. Natynczyk in his letter dated 29 January, 2010 confirms that it was Maj. Salsman who diagnosed the need for special boots for this young Canadian Forces female member due to her Plantar Fasciitis [pes planus] "and that his recommendation was accepted and acted upon immediately" [see Appendix 23].

Unfortunately, for old "Uncle Walt" [General W.Z. Natynczyk], these special boots to accommodate this young female Canadian Force member's plantar fasciitis were never given to her!!

Yet, old "Uncle Walt" [General W.Z. Natynczyk] nevertheless concluded "I am satisfied that you [this young Canadian Forces female member] have been treated appropriately" [see Appendix 23].

What?

As mentioned, is "Uncle Walt" 'out to lunch'?

This was expressed in a letter by this young female Canadian Force member's letter dated 13 February, 2010 to none other than the Chief Commissioner of the Canadian Human Rights Commission, Jennifer Lynch, 344 Slater Street, 8th Floor, Ottawa, Ontario, Canada K1A 1E1 [see Appendix 29].

As this young female Canadian Force member stated:

"Specifically, Quote #6 - page 4: General W.Z. Natynczyk in his letter dated 29 January, 2010 confirms that it was Maj. Salsman who diagnosed the need for special boots for me due to my Plantar Fasciitis [pes planus] "and that his recommendation was accepted and acted upon immediately".

This is NOT ACCURATE, in fact I was NEVER issued these boots to correct my disability of Bilateral Pes Planus & Posterior tibial dysfunction level 1 instead, I was released [fired] from the Canadian Forces" [see Appendix 29].

Wow, what to do?

It was quite obvious that old "Uncle Walt" [General W.Z. Natynczyk] statement "and that his recommendation was accepted and acted upon immediately" [see Appendix 23] was not accurate, this young female Canadian Force member never did receive those special boots to accommodate her plantar fasciitis [see her letter to the Canadian Human Rights Commission – Appendix 29].

Well, as far as the Canadian Forces were concerned, let's try to correct that problem with another apparent fabrication?

Specifically, let's add the false statement by Canadian Forces Commander Y. Couture, National Defense Headquarters, in a letter dated 7 July, 2010 to the Canadian Human Rights Commission [agent Kathryn Lavery] who said this young female Canadian Forces member was not issued the corrective boots by her Nanaimo, British Columbia, Canada 748 Comm Unit because she "had already commenced her release proceedings" [see Appendix 27].

Another apparent outright fabrication ["lie"] by the Canadian Forces?

You bet?

In actual fact, this young female Canadian Forces member had been fired [released in spite of her protests] by the commanding officer of her Nanaimo, British Columbia, Canada 748 Comm Unit, that being Captain D.R. Bowhey.

Chapter 22

Gaston Boisvert of the Canadian Human Rights Commission states we will not be addressing the substance of the complaint?

As mentioned, when it became very obvious to this young female Canadian Forces member that the internal grievance process was nothing but a sham, especially with old "Uncle Walt" [General W.Z. Natynczyk] statement "and that his recommendation was accepted and acted upon immediately" [see Appendix 23] which was not an accurate statement, this young female Canadian Force member never did receive those special boots to accommodate her plantar fasciitis, she wrote a letter dated 13 February, 2010 to the Chief Commissioner, Jennifer Lynch, of the Canadian Human Rights Commission [Appendix 29].

It appears that the Chief Commissioner, Jennifer Lynch, of the Canadian Human Rights Commission apparently [conveniently] misplaced her letter [see Appendix 30].

In any event, would the Canadian Human Rights Commission hear this young female Canadian Forces member's complaint of discrimination based on being diagnosed with plantar fasciitis by the Canadian Forces but not given the special boots necessary so she could perform her military duties?

After all, remember these findings:

Specifically, Quote #1 - page 3: General W.Z. Natynczyk in his letter dated 29 January, 2010 confirms that this young Canadian Forces female member's Plantar Fasciitis [pes planus] is congenital "your foot condition is congenital" [see Appendix 23].

Specifically, Quote #2 - page 4: General W.Z. Natynczyk in his letter dated 29 January, 2010 confirms that because this young Canadian Forces female member had a congenital condition of Plantar Fasciitis she was qualified for orthopaedic footwear according to Canadian Forces Supply Manual "Veteran Affairs Canada defines pes planus, the genetic condition from which you suffer, as a deformed foot. As such, you qualified to be fitted with orthopaedic footwear" [see Appendix 23].

Specifically, Quote #3 - page 3: General W.Z. Natynczyk in his letter dated 29 January, 2010 confirms that because this young Canadian Forces female member had a congenital condition of Plantar Fasciitis she was qualified for orthopaedic footwear according to Canadian Forces Supply Manual and that, as stated in the Canadian Forces Supply Manual that if improper footwear is given (to a soldier recruit) "improper fitted footwear affects the general well being of an individual, often to such an extent as to impair health, morale and efficiency. It is, therefore, of the utmost importance that individuals wear footwear for which they have been measured and properly fitted" [see Appendix 23].

Specifically, Quote #4 - page 3: General W.Z. Natynczyk in his letter dated 29 January, 2010 confirms that "I find that the boot fitting procedures set out in the supply manual were not followed by supply personnel at 748 Comm Sqn, Nanaimo" with regard to this young Canadian Forces female member [see Appendix 23].

Specifically, Quote #5 - page 4: General W.Z. Natynczyk in his letter dated 29 January, 2010 confirms that it was Maj. Salsman who diagnosed the need for special boots for this young Canadian Forces female member due to her Plantar Fasciitis [pes planus] "I find the earliest opportunity at which you could have been assessed as requiring orthopaedic footwear was upon examination by Maj. Salsman" [see Appendix 23].

Specifically, on 10 July, 2006 Canadian Forces Shilo Base Surgeon Major Salsman ordered special boots for this young Canadian Forces female member so she could perform her military duties [see Appendix 12].

Remember, instead of being given these special boots to accommodate her plantar fasciitis, the commanding officer of her Nanaimo, British Columbia, Canada 748 Comm Unit, that being Captain D.R. Bowhey, fired this young Canadian Forces female member.

Well, would Chief Commissioner, Jennifer Lynch, of the Canadian Human Rights Commission do anything to correct this discrimination [plantar fasciitis] for this young female Canadian Forces member?

You guessed it, no way!

Not now!

Not ever!

As cited by her agent, Gaston Boisvert, Early Resolution Team Leader, Canadian Human Rights Commission, 344 Slater Street, 8th Floor, Ottawa, Ontario, Canada K1A 1E1 in a letter dated 19 March, 2010, he made it very clear the Canadian Human Rights Commission was not going to deal with this young female Canadian Forces member's discrimination complaint about plantar fasciitis and not being accommodated by the Canadian Forces [see Appendix 31].

As this Canadian Human Rights Commission Gaston Boisvert states:

"Please note that the Commission will not be addressing the substance of the complaint at this time, i.e., it will not be considering evidence to the allegations of discrimination" [see Appendix 31].

What?

The Canadian Human Rights Commission headed by Chief Commissioner, Jennifer Lynch, would NOT be addressing "the substance of this young female Canadian Force member's human rights complaint"?

Chapter 23

According to Kathryn Lavery of the Canadian Human Rights Commission complaining about "clown sized combat boots" is frivolous – what a moron!

Well, if the Canadian Human Rights Commission will not be addressing this young female Canadian Forces member's discrimination complaint about plantar fasciitis and not being accommodated by the Canadian Forces, then what would the Canadian Human Rights Commission be doing for her?

Again, as cited by Gaston Boisvert of the Canadian Human Rights Commission in his letter dated 19 March, 2010, Gaston Boisvert incredibly states the Canadian Human Rights Commission "review will be limited to issues raised under section 41(1)(d)" [see Appendix 31].

Well, what does section 41(1)(d) address?

It simply looks at whether or not a complaint is "trivial, frivolous, vexatious or made in bad faith."

What?

Would anyone say that this young female Canadian Forces member's discrimination complaint was "trivial, frivolous, vexatious or made in bad faith?"

Don't bother answering that if you work for the Federal Government of Canada?

Let's see what Kathryn Lavery, agent for the Canadian Human Rights Commission, used in her 9 June, 2010 section 40/41 review to determine if this young female Canadian Forces member's discrimination complaint was "trivial, frivolous, vexatious or made in bad faith?"

Well, on page 6 of Canadian Human Rights Commission Kathryn Lavery's 9 June, 2010 report, it's clear what the Canadian Forces told her:

"The CF submits that the complaint is both trivial and frivolous ... nor does it raise any issues of public interest" [see Appendix 32].

Hmm, doesn't raise any issues of public interest?

Is that true?

Not really!

Why would the Canadian Forces say that?

The possible reason, how many people suffer from plantar fasciitis?

What would it cost to equip all those with plantar fasciitis who wanted to join the Canadian Forces or any other Canadian Government department for that matter?

Was cost a factor in 'kyboshing' this young female Canadian Forces member's discrimination complaint to Chief Commissioner, Jennifer Lynch, of the Canadian Human Rights Commission?

Was it simply a matter of money to ignore this young female Canadian Forces member's discrimination complaint?

After all, in a study of 3600 Canadian Army recruits, Harris and Beath found a 2% incidence of spastic (rigid) flatfoot and a 6% incidence of flexible flatfoot.[1]

That's quite a handful of potential plantar fasciitis sufferers?

Especially if people like this young female Canadian Forces member's discrimination complaint had been looked at seriously by either the Canadian Forces or the Canadian Human Rights Commission.

That may have proven to be a lot of purchases of special boots to accommodate all those plantar fasciitis sufferers, or possibly potential out of court settlements had only a fraction of them sued the Canadian Government or Canadian Armed Forces in Federal Court they were not accommodated by this special equipment to meet their disability.

This young female Canadian Forces member's discrimination complaint not in public interest, as both the Canadian Forces and the Canadian Human Rights Commission contended?

Baloney?

However, what was Canadian Human Rights Commission Kathryn Lavery's conclusion, appearing on page 10 of her report?

Surprise, surprise?

You guessed it?

Canadian Human Rights Commission Kathryn Lavery's conclusion, appearing on page 10 of her report:

"It would not be in the public interest for the Commission to deal with this complaint" [see Appendix 33].

I don't think so?

That wasn't the real reason?

Had this young female Canadian Force member's discrimination complaint been taken seriously by the Canadian Forces and the Canadian Human Rights Commission, it would not have been in the interests of the Canadian Government or the Canadian Forces because they would have had to fork out for special equipment for plantar fasciitis sufferers or suffer the consequences – possibly suits against them.

A factor of money, you bet?

As cited:

"Custom orthotics are usually made by taking a plaster cast or an impression of the individual's foot and then constructing an insert specifically designed to control biomechanical risk factors such as pes planus, valgus heel alignment and discrepancies in leg length. In one study, orthotics were cited by 27 percent of patients as the best treatment."[2]

As also cited:

"The main disadvantage of orthotics is the cost, which may range from $75 to $300 or more and which is frequently not covered by health insurance."[3]

In fact, if you look at this young female Canadian Forces member's discrimination complaint request, it requests reimbursement for her orthotics, which totaled $330 [see Appendix 37].

Add this amount to each Canadian Forces recruit needing such orthotics because of plantar fasciities, and that's one chunk of money!

No wonder the Canadian Forces, the Canadian Government and the Canadian Human Rights Commission didn't really want to look at her discrimination complaint?

Footnotes

1. Harris RI, Beath T. Etiology of peroneal spastic flat foot. J Bone Joint Surg Br. 1948;30:624–34.

2. Wolgin M, Cook C, Graham C, Mauldin D. Conservative treatment of plantar heel pain: long-term follow-up. Foot Ankle Int. 1994;15:97–102

3. Kwong PK, Kay D, Voner RT, White MW. Plantar fasciitis. Mechanics and pathomechanics of treatment. Clin Sports Med. 1988;7:119–26.

Also reference to: Treatment of Plantar Fasciitis
Craig C. Young, M.D., Medical College of Wisconsin, Milwaukee, Wisconsin
Darin S. Rutherford, M.D., Mercy Sports Medicine, Janesville, Wisconsin
Mark W. Niedfelt, M.D., Medical College of Wisconsin, Milwaukee, Wisconsin.
Am Fam Physician. 2001 Feb 1;63(3):467-475

Chapter 24

Kathryn Lavery of the Canadian Human Rights Commission ignores the lies by Canadian Forces Shilo Base Surgeon Major Salsman and General W.Z. Natynczyk to deny the young female soldier justice!

Well, let's see what else Kathryn Lavery, agent for the Canadian Human Rights Commission, used in her 9 June, 2010 section 40/41 review to determine if this young female Canadian Forces member's discrimination complaint was "trivial, frivolous, vexatious or made in bad faith?"

Well, on page 9 and on page 10 of Canadian Human Rights Commission Kathryn Lavery's 9 June, 2010 report, it's clear she put much weight in Canadian Forces' "independent" grievance conclusion [see Appendix 33].

Remember, unfortunately for Canadian Human Rights Commission Kathryn Lavery, we've already seen that this Canadian Forces' "independent" grievance process was flawed:

In spite of this: Quote #1 - page 3: General W.Z. Natynczyk in his letter dated 29 January, 2010 confirms that this young Canadian Forces female member's Plantar Fasciitis [pes planus] is congenital "your foot condition is congenital" [see Appendix 23].

In spite of this: Quote #2 - page 4: General W.Z. Natynczyk in his letter dated 29 January, 2010 confirms that because this young Canadian Forces female member had a congenital condition of Plantar Fasciitis she was qualified for orthopaedic footwear according to Canadian Forces Supply Manual "Veteran Affairs Canada defines pes planus, the genetic condition from which you suffer, as a deformed foot. As such, you qualified to be fitted with orthopaedic footwear" [see Appendix 23].

In spite of this: Quote #3 - page 3: General W.Z. Natynczyk in his letter dated 29 January, 2010 confirms that because this young Canadian Forces female member had a congenital condition of Plantar Fasciitis she was qualified for orthopaedic footwear according to Canadian Forces Supply Manual and that, as stated in the Canadian Forces Supply Manual that if improper footwear is given (to a soldier recruit) "improper fitted footwear affects the general well being of an individual, often to such an extent as to impair health, morale and efficiency. It is, therefore, of the utmost importance that individuals wear footwear for which they have been measured and properly fitted" [see Appendix 23].

In spite of this: Quote #4 - page 3: General W.Z. Natynczyk in his letter dated 29 January, 2010 confirms that "I find that the boot fitting procedures set out in the supply manual were not followed by supply personnel at 748 Comm Sqn, Nanaimo" with regard to this young Canadian Forces female member [see Appendix 23].

In spite of this: Quote #5 - page 4: General W.Z. Natynczyk in his letter dated 29 January, 2010 confirms that it was Maj. Salsman who diagnosed the need for special boots for this young Canadian Forces female member due to her Plantar Fasciitis [pes planus] "I find the earliest opportunity at which you could have been assessed as requiring orthopaedic footwear was upon examination by Maj. Salsman" [see Appendix 23].

In spite of this: On 10 July, 2006 Canadian Forces Shilo Base Surgeon Major Salsman ordered special boots for this young Canadian Forces female member so she could perform her military duties [see Appendix 12].

In spite of this: On 05 July, 2006 the medical unit at Shilo Manitoba base camp recorded "blisters and hot spots" on left and right foot -- Signed by Canadian Forces Shilo Base Surgeon Major Salsman [See Appendix 8].

In spite of this: Also recorded in the medical unit at Shilo Manitoba base camp on 05 July, 2006 "on left foot there is a 1" long friction mark on the posterior aspect of the foot slightly proximal from the 'calcaneus(?)'. There is also a blister on the plantar aspect of the foot located on the heel. It appears to be relatively deep. On the right foot there is a similar friction mark as described on the left foot. There are hot spots located on the bottom of both heels" -- Signed by Canadian Forces Shilo Base Surgeon Major Salsman [see Appendix 8].

In spite of this: As also recorded in the medical unit at Shilo Manitoba base camp on 05 July, 2006 "friction marks, hot spots and blisters caused by grossly oversized combat boots" -- Signed by Canadian Forces Shilo Base Surgeon Major Salsman [see Appendix 8].

In spite of this: As also recorded in the medical unit at Shilo Manitoba base camp on 05 July, 2006 "enquire about new boots, should be fitted with orthotics, and dressed friction marks, dressed with 'hypafix(?)' and 'mepore(?)' -- Signed by Canadian Forces Shilo Base Surgeon Major Salsman [see Appendix 8].

In spite of this: It was also at this time that Canadian Forces Shilo Base Surgeon Major Salsman gave this young Canadian Forces female member a pamphlet on plantar fasciitis [see Appendix 9].

In spite of this: Also recorded in the medical unit at Shilo Manitoba base camp on 05 July, 2006 specific instructions that this young Canadian Forces female member should not drill, not march, not run, and no ruck or webbing marches [see Appendix 10].

In spite of this: Again, as recorded on 07 July, 2006 specific instructions for this young Canadian Forces female member indicated she should not drill, not march, and no ruck or webbing marches and this time no prolonged standing for more than 20 minutes [see Appendix 11].

In spite of this: The end result, this young Canadian Forces female member was taken from her BMQ course and admitted to Brandon Regional Health Centre on 13 July, 2006 with an infected toe because of the grossly oversized boots she had been issued by my 748 Comm unit "area around blister reddened … pus" [see Appendix 13].

In spite of this: As recorded in the medical unit at Shilo Manitoba base camp on 14 July, 2006 it indicated that this young Canadian Forces female member had been "in emergency last night" and then referred to "blister infected right foot" [see Appendix 14].

In spite of this: This young Canadian Forces female member was prescribed an antibiotic for her infected foot [see Appendix 15].

Yet, old "Uncle Walt" [General W.Z. Natynczyk] nevertheless concluded "I am satisfied that you [this young Canadian Forces female member] have been treated appropriately" [see Appendix 23].

In addition, old "Uncle Walt" [General W.Z. Natynczyk] added apparent fabrication with: Quote #6 - page 4: General W.Z. Natynczyk in his letter dated 29 January, 2010 confirms that it was Maj. Salsman who diagnosed the need for special boots for this young Canadian Forces female member due to her Plantar Fasciitis [pes planus] "and that his recommendation was accepted and acted upon immediately" [see Appendix 23].

Unfortunately, for old "Uncle Walt" [General W.Z. Natynczyk], these special boots to accommodate this young female Canadian Force member's plantar fasciitis were never given to her!

Yet, old "Uncle Walt" [General W.Z. Natynczyk] nevertheless concluded "I am satisfied that you [this young Canadian Forces female member] have been treated appropriately" [see Appendix 23].

Not surprising, what was Canadian Human Rights Commission Kathryn Lavery's conclusion, appearing on page 10 of her report:

"It would not be in the public interest for the Commission to deal with this complaint" [see Appendix 33].

Absolute baloney!

And what did the Canadian Human Rights Commission decide, not surprising too as cited in a decision dated 25 August, 2010 by David Langtry, Deputy Canadian Human Rights Commissioner:

"Not to deal with the complaint … because the complaint was "trivial, frivolous, vexatious or made in bad faith" [see Appendix 34].

Again, absolute baloney!

And incredibly, if this young female Canadian Forces member wanted to have this 'idiotic' Canadian Human Rights Commission decision reviewed by the Federal Court of Canada, David Langtry, Deputy Canadian Human Rights Commissioner in a letter dated 10 September, 2010 made it very clear that the Canadian Human Rights Commission "cannot be a respondent in a judicial review of its own decision" [see Appendix 35].

Wow, what a scam?

Are you following this?

Although this young female Canadian Forces member made a discrimination complaint to the Canadian Human Rights Commission, this was the end result.

The Canadian Human Rights Commission was not going to look at the underlying evidence of discrimination in this young female Canadian Forces member's discrimination complaint to the Canadian Human Rights Commission [as cited in Canadian Human Rights Commission Gaston Boisvert's 19 March, 2010 letter, see Appendix 31]?

Instead, the Canadian Human Rights Commission was going to accept carte blanche the decision of the Canadian Forces' "independent" grievance process as per Canadian Human Rights Commission Kathryn Lavery's 9 June, 2010 report [see Appendix 33]?

And, if this young female Canadian Forces member wanted to have the Federal Court of Canada review the Canadian Human Rights Commission's 'idiotic' decision that her complaint was "trivial, frivolous, vexatious or made in bad faith" [see Appendix 34], the Canadian Human Rights Commission could not be dragged into the judicial review of their own decision [as clearly cited in Deputy Canadian Human Rights Commissioner David Langtry's letter dated 10 September, 2010 - see Appendix 35].

What baloney?

And that's what you can expect from the Canadian Government, one Canadian Government department supporting another Canadian Government department at any cost.

And, don't worry the Federal Court of Canada will get in the picture too and they will do their best to protect their fellow Canadian Government departments, in this case the Canadian Human Rights Commission where this Canadian Government department as the Federal Court has ruled cannot not be dragged into the judicial review of it's own decision [as again clearly cited in Deputy Canadian Human Rights Commissioner David Langtry's letter dated 10 September, 2010 - see Appendix 35].

In other words, the Canadian Human Rights Commission does not have to defend their 'idiotic' decision(s)?

What a country?

Blocked this young female Canadian Forces member's discrimination complaint to the Canadian Human Rights Commission every which way?

How many other Canadian citizens have experienced this tripe?

Why to the detriment of this young female Canadian Forces member who obviously had a legitimate complaint of discrimination from the Canadian Forces?

Why?

Simply because it appears that cost may have been the factor in 'kyboshing' this young female Canadian Forces member's discrimination complaint to Chief Commissioner, Jennifer Lynch, of the

Canadian Human Rights Commission?

After all, as stated, 14.7% suffered foot problems (Plantar fasciitis, 1st MTP irritation, fat pad irritation).[1]

After all, this number of 14.7% could mean we are talking about a lot of orthotic insoles or special boots for the Canadian Forces?

As mentioned, had this young female Canadian Force member's discrimination complaint been taken seriously by the Canadian Forces and the Canadian Human Rights Commission, it would not have been in the interests of the Canadian Government or the Canadian Forces because they would have had to "fork out" for special equipment for plantar fasciitis sufferers or suffer the consequences – possibly suits against them.

A factor of money, you bet!

As again cited:

"The main disadvantage of orthotics is the cost, which may range from $75 to $300 or more and which is frequently not covered by health insurance."[2]

Again, if you look at this young female Canadian Forces member's discrimination complaint, she requested reimbursement for her orthotics, which came out to be $330.

Add this amount to each Canadian Forces recruit needing such orthotics because of plantar fasciities, and that's one chunk of money!

No wonder the Canadian Forces, the Canadian Government and the Canadian Human Rights Commission didn't really want to look at her discrimination complaint!

Footnotes

1. Canadian Forces Health Services Centre Physiotherapy Department

2. Kwong PK, Kay D, Voner RT, White MW. Plantar fasciitis. Mechanics and pathomechanics of treatment. Clin Sports Med. 1988;7:119–26.

Chapter 25

Another "idiot" with the Canadian Human Rights, David Langtry denies young female soldier justice because he considers running shoes are appropriate instead of proper fitting combat boots – what a "moron"?

That appears to be a pretty good scam the Canadian Government apparently pulls to ignore "discrimination"?

Have a buffer.

A so called "impartial" board that comes up with "gibberish"?

And then have the CHRC use that "gibberish" to not even look at the discrimination that has occurred?

Kathryn Lavery, agent for the Canadian Human Rights Commission, used in her 9 June, 2010 section 40/41 review to determine if this young female Canadian Forces member's discrimination complaint was "trivial, frivolous, vexatious or made in bad faith" [see Appendix 33] and cited in a decision dated 25 August, 2010 by David Langtry, Deputy Canadian Human Rights Commissioner: "not to deal with the complaint … because the complaint was trivial, frivolous, vexatious or made in bad faith" [see Appendix 34].

Both Lavery and Langtry apparently felt that the rationales used by the Canadian Forces to indicate this young female Canadian Forces member was well treated by the Canadian Forces was their ["rather stupid"] comment that she was allowed to use running shoes to complete her BMQ [see Appendix 33 for Lavery's comment as well as Appendix 36 for Langtry's comment] and that this was sufficient in dealing with this young female Canadian Forces member's plantar fasciitis?

What?

Again, apparently these Canadian Force "Einstein's" and Canadian Human Rights Commission "Einstein's" didn't realize that wearing running shoes apparently increases the pain and damage caused by plantar fasciitis?

As cited[1]:

"Anthony (1987) reported that running shoes should be considered protective devices (from dangerous or painful objects) rather than corrective devices, as their capacity for shock absorption and control of over-pronation is limited."[2]

"The modern running shoe and footwear generally reduce sensory feedback, apparently without diminishing injury-inducing impact–a process Robbins and Gouw (1991) described as the "perceptual illusion" of athletic footwear."[3]

"A resulting false sense of security may contribute to the risk of injury (Robbins and Gouw, 1991)."[4]

Again, the conclusions were:

"Running in shoes appears to increase the risk of plantar fasciitis and other chronic injuries of the lower limb by modifying the transfer of shock to muscles and supporting structures."[5]

Also, changing to running shoes is not a panacea remedy.

As cited:

"In general, plantar fasciitis is a self-limiting condition."[6]

"Unfortunately, the time until resolution is often six to 18 months, which can lead to frustration for patients and physicians."[7]

"Rest was cited by 25 percent of patients with plantar fasciitis in one study as the treatment that worked best."[8]

Apparently these Canadian Force "Einstein's" and Canadian Human Rights Commission "Einstein's" ignored the comments by "Uncle Walt" and that of studies in the field, such as those cited, where plantar fasciitis is "self-limiting" where six to 18 months is required to resolve, and rest is one of the prescribed treatments.[9]

"Uncle Walt's" pertinent comments were:

Specifically, Quote #2 - page 4: General W.Z. Natynczyk in his letter dated 29 January, 2010 confirms that because this young Canadian Forces female member had a congenital condition of Plantar Fasciitis she was qualified for orthopaedic footwear according to Canadian Forces Supply Manual "Veteran Affairs Canada defines pes planus, the genetic condition from which you suffer, as a deformed foot. As such, you qualified to be fitted with orthopaedic footwear" [see Appendix 23].

Specifically, Quote #3 - page 3: General W.Z. Natynczyk in his letter dated 29 January, 2010 confirms that because this young Canadian Forces female member had a congenital condition of Plantar Fasciitis she was qualified for orthopaedic footwear according to Canadian Forces Supply Manual and that, as stated in the Canadian Forces Supply Manual that if improper footwear is given (to a soldier recruit) "improper fitted footwear affects the general well being of an individual, often to such an extent as to impair health, morale and efficiency. It is, therefore, of the utmost importance that individuals wear footwear for which they have been measured and properly fitted" [see Appendix 23].

How, then could this young Canadian Forces female member be expected to perform all of the tough, physical requirements of "boot camp" [BMQ], especially when she had been given "clown sized" boots by her Nanaimo 748 Comm Unit?

Specifically, Quote #4 - page 3: General W.Z. Natynczyk in his letter dated 29 January, 2010 confirms that "I find that the boot fitting procedures set out in the supply manual were not followed by supply personnel at 748 Comm Sqn, Nanaimo" with regard to this young Canadian Forces female member [see Appendix 23].

Was this the end of the discrimination against this young female Canadian Forces member?

You bet not?

Apparently not in Canada [see Part II].

Footnotes

1. Barefoot Running
Michael Warburton

2. Anthony RJ (1987). The functional anatomy of the running training shoe. Chiropodist, December, 451-459

3 – 4. Robbins SE, Gouw GJ (1991). Athletic footwear: unsafe due to perceptual illusions. Medicine and Science in Sports and Exercise 23, 217-224

5. Barefoot Running
Michael Warburton

6 – 8. Wolgin, M; Cook, C; Graham, C & Mauldin, D. Conservative treatment of plantar heel pain: long-term follow-up, Foot Ankle Int., 1994, 15, 97–102

9. Also reference to: Treatment of Plantar Fasciitis
Craig C. Young, M.D., Medical College of Wisconsin, Milwaukee, Wisconsin
Darin S. Rutherford, M.D., Mercy Sports Medicine, Janesville, Wisconsin
Mark W. Niedfelt, M.D., Medical College of Wisconsin, Milwaukee, Wisconsin.
Am Fam Physician. 2001 Feb 1;63(3):467-475

Chapter 26

Where there is one liar, there are others!

This part of the book hopefully has described the mean-spirited Canadian Government departments, in this case the Canadian Forces and the Canadian Human Rights Commission, when they thought they could run 'rough-shod' over this young female Canadian Forces member without apparent consequences?

This book is an attempt to highlight their apparent "conniving behavior" and their apparent fabrications ["lies"] to accomplish their "devious" task.

As far as the author is concerned, where these people have done it once … chances are they've done it before or will do it again.

Hopefully, this book may prove beneficial to anyone who finds themselves in similar circumstances as this young female Canadian Forces member.

If you think the mistreatment of this young female Canadian Forces member was bad, wait till you read about the next case involving, this time, a young male Canadian Forces member.

On a final note, this guy seemed to have a positive experience with the Canadian Forces?

As he cites:

"I'm curious how other people with these foot problems deal with staying fit and staying on courses?"[1]

"I did my BMQ and SQ this summer with the comm res in Shilo and had no clue before that time that I had flat feet. The CF dr that did my medical exam didn't say anything, my family dr has never said anything, and the most pain I'd had before starting BMQ was after standing long periods at work, almost never any pain in sports and I just attributed that to 'regular' pain."[2]

"The first couple weeks of BMQ when we were doing heavy drill like 8-10 hours a day really did my feet in."[3]

"I figured they were just breaking in and I'd get over the pain once they got used to the heavier schedule, so I just kept going until finally it became a major problem (ie I couldn't walk in the morning when we got up for PT, used the sides of my feet and had to throw my shoes on tie them tight and pretty much felt like I was sprinting during the entire jog regardless of pace).”[4]

“Went to the MIR, they gave me 2 or 3 days of LD, ordered me to get new running shoes with better arch support, and gave me some ibuprophene for the plantar fascitis I was experiencing as well.”[5]

“Really, for my first experience with the Forces hospital/dr system it was a very positive experience.”[6]

“Rather then the ‘suck it up buttercup’ attitude I expected it was like ‘You're hurting? Lets see if we can fix it’.”[7]

“They also gave me an appointment with the orthopedic specialist, but he wasn't full time and it took me almost 5 weeks of my 7 week course to see him. Got some bio-orthodic insoles made up and he told me I ‘had flat, over-flexible feet, and are suffering from plantar fasciitis’ and that basically it wasn't going to get better until I got off course and could take it easy on my feet a bit.”[8]

“I decided oh well, its just pain I'll move on and finish the course. Ended up with more wrong with my feet and basically all from the initial complication that they were flat and I had no clue until damage was done.”[9]

“So my question to everyone out there in the army with flat feet: What do you do to minimize pain and maximize your performance? Do you go to an orthopedic specialist at all? Did you put vibram soles on your boots and did they help?”[10]

Why the difference with this young female Canadian Forces member, was it because she complained?

Was it because she put in a grievance?

Was it because she put in a human rights complaint?

All the author can say is “suck it up Canadian Forces, let's not be so delicate?”

So the young female Canadian Forces put in a grievance and a human rights complaint?

You deserved the complaint?

After all, those that complain are highlighted for further abuse.

As cited:

"In 2006, Constable Luis Cerritos took stress leave due to workplace conditions that he claimed were rife with harassment, racism, bullying and physical intimidation."[11]

"I was being called names that I had never heard before. I started being ashamed of not being white".[12]

The harassment escalated when Cerritos lodged a complaint within the RCMP about the way he was treated. "My wife was pregnant at the time and my unborn baby was called a Mexican motherf----er".[13]

If nothing else, hopefully this book has highlighted the apparent vindictive behavior of the Canadian Government as an employer?

Then again, who wants to work for the Government of Canada, when it appears if you do so, one has to exchange your "soul" [ethics]?

Just look at the RCMP [Royal Canadian Mounted Police] and the DND [Department of National Defense]?

In the Dziekanski case, did the RCMP get away with murder?

Some appear to think yes?

"Nothing will happen to them, still they are on the job, the four RCMP officers who caused Robert's death by what they did, and then they lie," said Cisowski.[14]

The case involved the vicious tasering to death of 40-year-old Polish immigrant Robert Dziekanski.

The RCMP lies apparently started immediately.

Richmond RCMP Sgt. Pierre Lemaitre said officers struggled to subdue the man: 'Even though he had received what they call pulses, two pulses from Taser, he was still out of control.'[15]

The man actually died after 4 Taser jolts, witness alleges.[16]

In fact, one witness said she offered to tell the RCMP officers what she witnessed, and that one officer said, "'I'll be with you in a few minutes.'" But the officers did not take a statement from her, she alleges.[17]

As reported, "within seconds, he had been Tasered. Dziekanski, even after falling to the ground, shrieking in pain, was Tasered repeatedly."[18]

The cover-up begins!

"After the event, the Mounties all gave similar statements about how Dziekanski had come at them, yelling and wildly swinging the stapler, and how several officers had to wrestle the man to the ground."[19]

However, a video proves the RCMP officers outright lied!

A witness's video of the event showed none of that happened ... if not for the video, might have got away with whitewashing what the judge called the force's "shameful" conduct in the events that led to an innocent man's death.[20]

As further reported, "I saw more RCMP officers lie to cover up this cowardly crime."[21]

Incredibly, "on Dec. 12, 2008, B.C. Criminal Justice branch spokesman Stan Lowe "cleared" the four officers of any wrongdoing and portrayed Dziekanski as a violent and agitated alcoholic whose irrational behavior contributed to his own death."[22]

However, even this Stan Lowe was put in his place when Cisowski had the satisfaction of hearing Thomas Braidwood call the four Mounties "inappropriately aggressive" and "patently unbelievable," while emphasizing Dziekanski did nothing wrong nor in any way caused his own death.[23]

Caught in their lies thanks to videotape of the "cowardly" crime, as it has been described.

Braidwood called the bystander video by Paul Pritchard of Dziekanski's Tasering death "invaluable" evidence that "couldn't be cross-examined."[24]

"Onlookers were incredulous when RCMP Commissioner William Elliott said Friday he wouldn't be announcing any disciplinary measures for any of the four Mounties for their role in Dziekanski's death."[25]

Get away with murder and no consequences?

Even the apology to Robert Dziekanski's mother was a bunch of RCMP bunk?

"A raft of internal RCMP emails was released through an Access to Information Act request showing that the April 1 apology was a carefully-crafted script designed not to blame any RCMP member."[26]

"On the day before the staging of the apology, RCMP Deputy Commissioner Gary Bass reassured RCMP staff relations supervisor Brian Roach that their "apology" to Cisowski did not mean they were apologizing for anything specific that any of their officers had done."[27]

"Essentially, even though the word 'apology' worries some, we are not apologizing for the actions of specific members or saying anything about specific actions."[28]

Cisowski said yesterday "this just shows that the RCMP even when they apologize to me, they coverup."[29]

Actually tasered five times!

"The e-mail, sent by RCMP Chief Supt. Dick Bent to Assistant Commissioner Al Macintyre suggested for the first time that the four Mounties who responded to a call at Vancouver's airport planned to use a Taser on Robert Dziekanski, who died at the airport on Oct. 14, 2007, after he was Tasered five times."[30]

Footnotes

1 - 10. Flat Feet: training and army courses
Army.ca Forums News
December 15, 2004, 00:55:40

11. Power and change in the RCMP: The role of agency and structure in workplace bullying
Ruth B. McKay, Carleton University
Cristina Ciocirlan, Elizabethtown College
Paul Ngo, St. Nobert College

12 - 13. Gatehouse, J. and Charles G. (2007). What"s really killing the Mounties. Maclean"s, Vol. 120, (46). Accessed March 29th, 2009

14. 'Still they get no consequences'. By Suzanne Fournier, The Province,

June 20, 2010.

15 – 16. RCMP say deceased man was 40-year-old Polish immigrant Robert Dziekanski. Last Updated: Tuesday, October 16, 2007. CBC News.

17. One witness said she offered to tell the RCMP officers what she witnessed.

18 - 20. Inquiry deservedly hammers RCMP in Dziekanski death. By Paul Schneiderit, The Chronicle Herald, Tue. Jun 22.

21. I saw more RCMP officers lie to cover up this cowardly crime.

22 - 25. 'Still they get no consequences'. By Suzanne Fournier, The Province, June 20, 2010.

26 - 29. RCMP's apology grudging, evasive. By Suzanne Fournier, The Province, June 17, 2010.

30. E-mail Suggests Four RCMP Officers Committed Perjury While Senior Officers Sat Silent. Contributed on Sun, 2009/06/21 - 2:30pm.

Also see: Startling New Email Halts Inquiry. By Neal Hall and Lori Culbert; June 20, 2009 - Vancouver Sun.

Also see: Damning e-mail suggests the four officers committed perjury and that senior officers sat silent while they did. By Ian Mulgrew; June 20, 2009 - Vancouver Sun.

Chapter 27

Some more liars and their lies!

The case involving the vicious tasering to death of 40-year-old Polish immigrant Robert Dziekanski warrants an additional chapter to see the extent of the lies by some members of the RCMP to cover-up.

After all, if the RCMP can do it, why not some members of the Canadian Forces?

As noted, "we have seen often-quoted Mountie mouthpiece Cpl. Dale Carr tell the Braidwood inquiry that top RCMP brass made a deliberate decision not to correct misinformation RCMP had given to the media about Dziekanski's death."[1]

In fact, "e-mail suggests four RCMP Officers committed perjury while senior officers sat silent,"[2] specifically suggests Mounties planned to deploy Taser before they arrived at YVR, contrary to their testimony.[3]

As reported, "after months of outrage about the conduct of the four Mounties who responded to Vancouver Airport Oct. 14, 2007, who can believe that at the last minute, a federal lawyer would produce what many would consider a smoking gun -- an e-mail saying the officers decided to use the Taser before confronting the Polish immigrant?"[4]

"If true, the Nov. 5, 2007, e-mail titled "Media strategy -- release of the YVR video," from RCMP Chief Supt. Dick Bent to assistant commissioner Al McIntyre, establishes the four have been lying through their teeth. This critical document suggests the four officers committed perjury and that senior officers sat silent while they did so."[5]

"The documents that have just come to our attention include a critical e-mail from very high up in the RCMP chain of command, disclosing that the officers decided in a premeditated way, en route to the scene."[6]

Even the RCMP lawyers apparently lie?

"Lawyer Helen Roberts, who represents the RCMP at the inquiry, offered a tearful apology to inquiry commissioner Thomas Braidwood, a retired judge, for not disclosing the e-mail sooner."[7]

"Helen Roberts had every reason to be in tears Friday as she apologized to the public inquiry into Dziekanski's death for failing to disclose what appears to be not just germane but also startlingly important evidence."[8]

Robert's crocodile tears don't wash!

"If Roberts had cried over Dziekanski mother's pain, I would be moved -- but a veteran lawyer wet-eyed over another screw-up in this case? I think they were crocodile tears."[9]

"I find this delay in disclosing it to the commission appalling," Braidwood said. "The contents of this e-mail goes to the heart of this inquiry's work."[10]

"It should have been disclosed much, much sooner ... months and months ago."[11]

"It's a stunning turn of events," Don Rosenbloom, the lawyer representing the government of Poland at the inquiry.[12]

Rosenbloom said the 11th-hour disclosure "is totally inconsistent with testimony given under oath" and goes to the heart of the issue of police fabrication. During the hearing, he said, "we were alleging [the four Mounties] were fabricating their story."[13]

The RCMP fabrication was, in fact, true!

Dziekanski's mother told reporters she was surprised and angry about the e-mail being released so late. She suggested there had been a "coverup."[14]

"This is the kind of evidence someone should have known would have important consequences," said Walter Kosteckyj, the lawyer representing Dziekanski's mother at the inquiry.[15]

He said he had spent the last two weeks preparing his final arguments for the inquiry, only to find not all the evidence has been heard.[16]

The RCMP lawyer tries to white-wash the facts?

David Butcher, the lawyer representing Const. Bill Bentley, one of the four Mounties involved in the in-custody death, said Bent's e-mail was hearsay and not credible evidence.[17]

B.C. Attorney-General Mike de Jong said he was concerned about the new development, "the possibility that new evidence may be emerging at this late date is troubling, and I'm sure very troubling for the commission itself," he said.[18]

"Commissions of this sort, and really our system of justice, rely on all witnesses who give evidence under oath to provide truthful and honest answers."[19]

Incredibly, Commissioner William Elliott's carefully parsed press release was equally unbelievable: "This was simply an oversight. Unfortunately in an exercise of this magnitude, such an oversight can occur."[20]

Elliott a moron, as cited, "no one but a moron overlooks the import of an e-mail like this" [see Appendix 10a – 10c].[21]

That was not an "oversight." It was professional incompetence or a cover-up.[22]

Paul Kennedy, the chairman of the Commission for Public Complaints Against the RCMP, using a news conference in Vancouver, took some well-aimed verbal shots at stagnant RCMP culture, especially its notorious, self-destructive resistance to change. It is a "massively inert" organization, he said, and that must not stand.[23]

Footnotes

1. RCMP admissions in Dziekanski Taser death are troubling. By Damian Inwood, Wed, Apr 22 2009.

2. E-mail Suggests Four RCMP Officers Committed Perjury While Senior Officers Sat Silent. Contributed on Sun, 2009/06/21 - 2:30pm.

3. Startling New Email Halts Inquiry. By Neal Hall and Lori Culbert; June 20, 2009 - Vancouver Sun.

4 - 5. Damning e-mail suggests the four officers committed perjury and that senior officers sat silent while they did. By Ian Mulgrew; June 20, 2009 - Vancouver Sun.

6 - 7. Startling New Email Halts Inquiry. By Neal Hall and Lori Culbert; June 20, 2009 - Vancouver Sun.

8 - 9. Damning e-mail suggests the four officers committed perjury and that senior officers sat silent while they did. By Ian Mulgrew; June 20, 2009 - Vancouver Sun.

10 - 19. Startling New Email Halts Inquiry. By Neal Hall and Lori Culbert; June 20, 2009 - Vancouver Sun.

20 - 22. Damning e-mail suggests the four officers committed perjury and that senior officers sat silent while they did. By Ian Mulgrew; June 20, 2009 - Vancouver Sun.

23. RCMP watchdog goes out firing with Dziekanski report. Posted: December 08, 2009, 6:35 PM by Ron Nurwisah. By Brian Hutchinson, National Post.

Chapter 28

Let's look at some other liars and their lies!

Incredibly, in another high profile case, another senior RCMP officer lied again and again.

The so-called RCMP expert witness, classed an expert witness on blood-pattern analyses, was "accused of perjury and exposed in B.C. Supreme Court as the author of a flawed forensic report that got basic biology wrong."[1]

Who was this RCMP Officer?

"Staff Sgt. Ross Spenard's credibility was shredded during the recent second-degree murder trial of Charlie Rae Lincoln, an aboriginal woman convicted of stabbing to death her own two-year-old. He acknowledged misleading the court and failing to send a letter to the Crown in the case revealing the concerns about the report and his errors."[2]

RCMP Spenard thought he covered his tracks by shredding documents.

He was wrong.

As noted, "armed with a copy of documents that Spenard thought were destroyed, defense lawyer Matthew Nathanson forced him to make a series of devastating admissions."[3]

The document was riddled with so many DNA misinterpretations and errors that the top experts in the field were flown in from Edmonton and Halifax to correct it. Some conclusions were "not scientifically sound," they said.[4]

"You were not being truthful, right?" the lawyer said, confronting the Mountie with a transcript of his earlier testimony.[5]

"Yes, I agree" Spenard admitted.[6]

As emphasized, "the performance was as bad as any at the Braidwood inquiry into the death of Robert Dziekanski, which has also featured RCMP officers seemingly uncomfortable with the truth."[7]

"You will recall the Staff Sgt. Spenard gave some evidence of blood found in... [a] house at different places," the justice said before sending the jurors to deliberate. "You have heard the Crown totally ignore his evidence, and I suggest to you that you do ignore his evidence completely.[8]

"Staff. Sgt. Spenard is the perfect example of a person who clearly lied under oath, and violated his oath to tell the truth, and he even agreed to this. That conclusion is so clear and convincing, and so serious, that I suggest you should consider his evidence to be completely tainted, and without any value whatsoever."[9]

Footnotes

1 - 9. Caught in a web of documents he thought had been destroyed: Blood-splatter expert admits to misleading court and failing to send a letter to the Crown revealing concerns about the forensic report.
Ian Mulgrew, Vancouver Sun, June 29, 2009.

Chapter 29

How many victims reported his behavior to the Canadian Forces long before he was finally arrested?

Let's turn our attention to this case.

As cited:

"A commander who was a rising star in Canada's military pleaded guilty Monday to the murders of two women, the sexual assaults of two others and dozens of breaking and entering charges in which he stole panties from the bedrooms of girls as young as 11."[1]

"Col. Russell Williams, who once flew prime ministers and served as a pilot to Queen Elizabeth II during a visit, was the commander of Canada's largest Air Force base until he was charged earlier this year. He was photographed in January with Defense Minister Peter MacKay and Canada's top general during an inspection of a Canadian aircraft on its way to support relief efforts in Haiti. He is alleged to have killed his second victim just over a week after he appeared with MacKay."[2]

"He pleaded guilty Monday to two first-degree murder charges, two sexual assaults and 82 breaking and entering charges in a Belleville, Ontario court. The 47-year-old faces an automatic sentence of life in prison with no possibility for parole for at least 25 years."[3]

"Prosecutors said Williams targeted girls and women in their teens and 20s and often photographed himself in their underwear."[4]

"At the sentencing hearing following his guilty plea, prosecutors showed photographs of Williams wearing a 12-year-old girl's cartoon-decorated underwear, with his genitalia protruding from them, while he was lying on her bed."[5]

"Other photos showed him wearing underwear belonging to 11-year-old twins."[6]

"In some of the pictures he was masturbating."[7]

"People in the courtroom, many of them victims and their families, were in tears and appeared stunned."[8]

"Prosecutors also said Williams videotaped the assaults and murders."[9]

"He pleaded guilty to the murder of Jessica Lloyd, 27, whose body was found in February, and Marie Comeau, a 38-year-old corporal under his command who was found dead in her home last November. Both women were asphyxiated."[10]

As further reported:

"Whether his victims fought him off or complied with every perverted command he gave them, convicted sex killer Col. Russell Williams showed no mercy to the two women who begged for their lives before he brutally murdered them, court heard Tuesday."[11]

"The horrifying details came on the same day court heard Williams was in his 20s when he developed a fetish for stealing women's lingerie that would culminate in murder."[12]

"Williams repeatedly raped 37-year-old Comeau — who first caught his eye during a military VIP flight — after breaking into her home last November and striking her repeatedly in the head with a flashlight."[13]

"He paused only to re-adjust his cameras, or to reach for the device during the attack to get a close-up shot of the rape, the court heard."[14]

"After nearly two hours, Williams put a piece of duct tape over her nose, cutting off her air supply."[15]

As she slumped to the floor, court heard that Comeau made a final plea: "Have a heart please. I've been really good... I want to live."[16]

"She died and Williams turned off the camera."[17]

What a sick bastard?

As one person commented, "this is one sick Canadian bastard. I hope he burns in hell for ALL OF ETERNITY!"

Was this "rising star" ever psychologically assessed?

As further cited:

His next victim, 27-year-old Lloyd, did everything Williams asked of her in an effort not to "upset" him, the Crown said.[18]

"Williams broke into her Belleville home in January, tied her up and raped her repeatedly for hours."[19]

104

"Only this time, he fastened a black zip tie around her neck and took her to his Tweed home, where he repeated the torture."[20]

"Lloyd was so terrified she apologized when she failed to move into the sexual position Williams demanded. She even asked permission to lower her legs after he had raped her. It had no effect."[21]

"When she started to convulse from a seizure, in extreme distress and begging for help, he calmly walked to his camera to turn it on."[22]

At one point, Lloyd pleads: "If I die, will you make sure my mom knows that I love her."[23]

"That heart-wrenching detail, read aloud in court, left many in the room sobbing loudly."[24]

"Lloyd's ordeal — which lasted almost an entire day — is documented in photos and on videotape. He even snapped a photo of her body after he has struck her and strangled her with rope, the blood from the wound pooling near her head."[25]

"Once a rising star in the Canadian Armed Forces, Williams has become an outcast whose depraved actions have rocked the military to its core."[26]

Again, what a dirty bastard this "rising star" was?

Because this guy was a "rising star", how long did the Canadian Forces cover-up this guy's indiscretions?

Surely, someone must have complained about him and / or his behavior?

Again, was this bastard ever psychologically assessed?

Are the psychologists the Canadian Forces employ well qualified?

In one particular case, it appears that a psychologist that works for the RCMP now used to apparently work for the DND.

It appears that, instead of the required APA [American Psychological Association] and / or CPA [Canadian Psychology Association] accredited program, this guy graduated from some other program?

As cited:

"Every one knows that if they want to make psychology a career goal, one has to obtain a recognized degree from a properly approved university."[27]

The standard for America is a degree program that has been approved by the American Psychological Association and in Canada the degree program has to be approved by the Canadian Psychological Association.

In terms of at least one 'psychologist' employed by the RCMP[28], his diploma when he received it had neither approval.[29]

In other words, this RCMP 'psychologist' who is accessing RCMP applicants in terms of their suitability has a diploma that is neither approved by the American Psychological Association nor by the Canadian Psychological Association.

One young clean-cut RCMP applicant[30] actually questioned this guy's credentials:

RECEIVED
MAY 3 1 2010
D Division HSO
25 May, 2010
Neil Anderson
Newly contracted RCMP Psychologist
Health Services Offices
D Division Headquarters:
1091 Portage Avenue
P.O. Box 5650
Winnipeg, MB R3C 3K2
Mr. Anderson,
I noticed that you are cited as having a Ph.D. in Clinical Psychology from Pacifica Graduate Institute (Carpinteria, California), however, aren't their programs not approved by the APA because of the distance component in them and their programs are definitely not CP A approved and if not APA or CP A approved are their degrees up to par?
Given this, I will have to question your interview with myself that occurred on 7 May at R.C.M.P., 754 Dominion, Winnipeg, MB.
Thank you

The young recruit did not receive a reply to his 25 May, 2010 letter from this guy, Neal Anderson!

You would think the RCMP [and the DND as he apparently used to work for them too] would have chosen someone with an APA or CPA approved degree?

What kind of psychologist assessed the "rising star" for the Canadian Forces, Col. Russell Williams?

Footnotes

1 – 10. Canadian Air Force star admits killing 2 women
He pleads guilty in their deaths, assaults on 2 others and 82 break-ins
By Charmaine Noronha, The Associated Press
2010-10-18

11 – 26. Col. Williams showed no mercy as murder victims begged for their lives
By: Maria Babbage, The Canadian Press
Latest NewsThe Canadian Press - ONLINE EDITION
Posted: 19/10/2010

Also see: "This is one sick Canadian bastard. I hope he burns in hell for ALL OF ETERNITY!" cited in: Canadian military officer exposed as serial killer, Tuesday 19th October, 2010

27. The Very Thin Red Line: This police force is "horribly" broken. Amazon.com.

28. Reference to: RCMP Contracts Over $10,000

Dr. Neal D. Anderson (Ph.D., C. Psych.) is a registered clinical psychologist in private practice in Manitoba. He has a Ph.D. in Clinical Psychology from Pacifica Graduate Institute (Carpinteria, California). Reference to:

29. This 'psychologist' has his diploma from Pacifica Graduate Institute which is neither approved by the American Psychological Association nor by the Canadian Psychological Association.

PACIFICA: are you approved??
From: Wendy Overend (WOverend@pacifica.edu)
Sent: May 13, 2010 10:55:59 AM
To: thegoodones@
Pacifica has applied to APA for consideration. Please keep an eye on our website for news and updates on the APA application process. APA is only applicable to the Ph.D. Clinical Psychology program... which is full-time low residency and NOT a hybrid distance learning program. Please sign up online if you are interested in receiving our materials! Thanks, Wendy

WOverend@pacifica.edu

Again, as of 15 August, 2010 Pacifica Graduate Institute confirms again that they are not APA approved, with the statement *"the Pacifica continues to update its Self-Study for application to the American Psychological Association for accreditation."* In other words, Pacifica Graduate Institute is not APA approved.

30. Reference to RCMP Application # A00184954 obtained under Privacy Access:
A search of Canada's security and intelligence agency [CSIS] found no criminal record or any record about the young 22 year old applicant:
Applicant Security Form   Page 1 of 1
Personnel Security (RCMP) > Personnel Security > CSIS Response
Applicant |D;A00184954
Application Status: Active   Location: D0026
Security Screening Request No.: 170067878
CSIS Result Code: 1   No Reportable Traces
Comments
CASE CONCLUDED WITHOUT FIELD INVESTIGATION. 2010-02-24

Postscript

Just look at their "rising star" Russell Williams [see Chapter 29]?

How many victims reported his behavior to the Canadian Forces long before he was finally arrested?

Should the victims or their families sue the Government of Canada and the Canadian Forces?

You bet they should?

This book has hopefully described the "mean-spirited" Canadian Government departments, in this case the Canadian Forces and the Canadian Human Rights Commission, when they thought they could run 'rough-shod' over this young female Canadian Forces member without consequences.

The book has hopefully made clear that it is not about a peeved female "grunt" but a concerted effort by the Government of Canada, in particular the Canadian Forces and the Canadian Human Rights Commission in their "tag-team" effort to not deal with her legitimate human rights complaint of discrimination due to her plantar fasciitis where the Canadian Human Rights Commission made it perfectly clear they were by-passing the content of her complaint to class it as "frivolous" to help the Canadian Forces out.

To add to the "mean-spirited" nature of the Canadian Forces and the Canadian Human Rights Commission in their "tag-team" effort to not deal with her human rights complaint that the Canadian Forces were not processing her 2009 re-application contrary to human rights doctrine.

People are tired of the tricks by the Federal Government of Canada to protect itself from legitimate complaints.

As a consequence, this book is an attempt to highlight the "conniving behavior" and apparent fabrication(s) ["lies"] to accomplish their "devious" task.

As far as the author is concerned and, as mentioned, where these people have done it once ... chances are they've done it before or will do it again.

This book may prove beneficial to anyone who finds themselves in similar circumstances as this young female Canadian Forces member and this young male Canadian Forces member.

As far as the author is concerned and, if nothing else, this book hopefully demonstrates that the Canadian Government appears to be a very "vindictive" employer?

The author knows that many people are disgruntled with the "crap" that goes on in our society.

However, the majority simply "throw their hands in the air" and say "can't fight city hall".

Sure you can!

Many "blog" their frustrations.

It's a good way to ventilate, but it's not a permanent record of the slights that people suffer.

The author's recommendation is that, if you get no satisfaction through regular channels, then write about the injustice.

There are many ways to economically publish your work nowadays.

Chapter 30

An open letter to Terry Mallenby
Canadian Human Rights File 20061409

Terry Mallenby, BA, BSW, MA
former federal peace officer
former Classification Officer BC Maximum Security Penitentiary
former Classification Officer BC Medium Security Mountain Prison
former Probation Officer NFLD Social Services Department
former Facility Operations Manager Whitbourne Youth Secure Custody

Dear Mr. Mallenby,

You are absolutely right.

I listened to the Military Doctor who lied!

I listened to the Military General who lied!

I didn't listen to the little guy's daughter whatsoever as payback because the little guy successfully sued my government!

Does this make an unethical person?

Signed

David Langtry
Canada's Human Rights Commissioner

Appendix 1 ["Regina profs pan free tuition for soldiers' kids]

Regina profs pan free tuition for soldiers' kids
Last Updated: Wednesday, March 24, 2010
CBC News

A scholarship program for the children of dead soldiers is raising
questions among some professors at the University of Regina.

They say they're concerned about Project Hero, a program that pays the
tuition of students who have had a parent die while on military duty for
Canada.

More than 80 universities and colleges in Canada have committed to the
project, which pays for four years of tuition, plus $1,000 for books.

U of R president Vianne Timmons announced two weeks ago the
university would provide the scholarship, but that has led to a campus
controversy.

Sixteen professors have signed a letter to Timmons stating the program
glorifies military action and they don't want their school to be part of it.

Among those with concerns is Jeffrey Webber, who teaches political
science and who says the name of the program celebrates military
intervention abroad.

"We think this is a glorification of the Afghan effort," he said.

Group proposes alternative
Webber said it's not that they are against helping the children of the
Canadian military.

"Why stop at the question of dependents of Canadian Forces personnel?
There's all kinds of people who are killed in workplace accidents," he
said.

As an alternative to the program, the group says there should be
universal access to post-secondary education.

The program was started about a year ago by Toronto businessman
Kevin Reed and retired general Rick Hillier.

"We just thought it was the right thing to do for these men and women in
uniform," said Reed, who's an honorary lieutenant-colonel of the

military's Canadian Brigade Group service units.

Story comments

March 30/10
Regarding Jeffrey Webber and friends opposing Project Hero is another example of academics who are ignorant to the realities of life and ungrateful to those that have fought for the freedom that they enjoy. \What a disgusting lot! The University of Regina could do better.

Do the children of these Prof's get free tuition? If so exactly WHY? What in God's name have these jokers done to deserve it. They make enough money sitting at their desks unlike a family which has lost it's bread winner serving this country. I sure hope these Prof's have not had any kids. The gene pool is simple being deluted if they have! I wonder if the female Prof's that signed it would like to go to a Taliban dominated area and try to teach. Now that I would really like to see, instead of them living here and working under the protection the men and women of the armed forces have provided for them. Send them all over their. They would be a lesser loss than a Canadian Forces member!

Appendix 2a [Canadian Forces to Attract Females]

Canadian Forces 2009 National Report
To the Committee for Women in NATO Forces (CWINF)

Policies and Initiatives Concerning Implementation of Gender
Mainstreaming

In keeping with its core values of freedom, democracy, Human Rights
and the rule of law, Canada is committed to the effective implementation
of UN Security Council Resolutions 1325 and 1820. Canada's efforts to
implement Resolutions 1325 and 1820 are linked to the overall
promotion and protection of equality and Human Rights for women and
girls within the framework of the 1995 Beijing Declaration and Platform
for Action, and its obligations under the Convention on the Elimination
of All Forms of Discrimination Against Women (CEDAW), the
Convention on the Rights of the Child, and other international human
rights instruments. Canada ensures that equality and Human Rights for
women and girls are integrated into its domestic and international
policies and programs. A number of Canada's federal government
departments including the Canadian Forces and Department of National
Defense (DND) are involved in the implementation of 1325 and 1820,
each with a specific area of responsibility.

Recruitment
The CF has introduced several measures to attract greater numbers of
qualified women from the Canadian workforce. Current activities
targeting potential female applicants range from local initiatives like
Recruiting Open Houses for women on International Women's Day,
participation in "Women in Leadership" career days and speaking
engagements at different universities in Canada where women leaders of
business and industry have the opportunity to discuss their own careers
with the leaders of tomorrow. At these latter venues, women in senior
military positions share their experiences and provide women with
important career information about the CF. Each major recruiting centre
has a designated Diversity Officer whose primary responsibility is to
liaise with key influencers in different groups and organizations. The
recruitment of women is a priority.

Appendix 2b [Harassment of Female Members in the Canadian Forces]

The Lived Experience of Women Veterans of the Canadian Forces
by
Sarah Louise Buydens
B.A., University of Victoria, 2002
A Thesis Submitted in Partial Fulfillment of the
Requirements for the Degree of
MASTERS OF ARTS
in the Department of Educational Psychology and Leadership Studies

what it is like to be a woman in the Canadian Forces - These studies have been funded by the Canadian Forces. Despite an emerging body of research about women and women"s roles in the military, to my knowledge no studies have explored the lived experiences of women in these military roles. I witnessed women military members navigate job-related stress and frequent gender based obstacles.

Research on women in nontraditional occupations, paramilitary work, and the American military highlight women face discrimination, sexual assault and harassment, multiple barriers, and gender related stress in these roles (J. M. Brown, 1998; J. Brown, Campbell, & Fife-Schaw, 1995; Lafontaine & Tredeau, 1986; Rosell, Miller, & Barber, 1995). Historically women have struggled to achieve pay and status equity and integration within the Canadian Forces (Dundas, 2000). Their triumphs have been echoed by multiple setbacks and barriers, culminating in the Canadian government forcing gender integration upon the military (Dundas). Entering these roles, women continued to face stereotypes, sexist attitudes, and lack of infrastructure to support them.

Human Rights Act – equality in the eyes of the law. The Canadian military had made changes to integrate women but it was the actions of the government that forced gender equality and further integration. The government created the Equality Rights section in April 1985 in the Canadian Human Rights Act (1985), granting all Canadians equal protection and benefit of the law without discrimination. Thus, the Canadian Forces was forced to open all trades and occupations to women.

Full integration of women into the Canadian Forces was not a smooth transition. Some servicewomen joined the Canadian Forces when historically they were stationed at static units and bases not required to participate in field units (Dundas, 2000). This change was not always a

114

welcome reality as the first report of the Minister"s Advisory Board on Women in the Canadian Forces noted senior naval servicewomen represented a "liability to serve at sea" (Dundas).

The commander of 1 Canadian Brigade compiled a list of concerns regarding integration of women. It is unknown how this list was developed and who else may have been involved in developing it. The list stated women lacked physical abilities to carry out duties, thereby, relying upon men to work harder and were not aggressive enough which compromised the Canadian Forces safety and effectiveness (Dundas, 2000).

Recipients of sexual harassment and gender based discriminatory behaviors report a range of psychological and physical symptoms, including anxiety, depression, fearfulness, insomnia, headaches, nausea, gastrointestinal disorders, irritability, anger, weight loss, uncontrolled crying, fatigue, and dental problems (Dansky & Kilpatrick, 1997; K. T. Schneider et al.).

The Canadian Forces is based on the team rather than the individual, and team cohesion is critical to operational effectiveness (Ahronson & Cameron, 2007). Group membership is vital to social and psychological functions, enhancing affect and psychological well-being (Cameron, 1999; Wright & Staw, 1999). Harassment and discrimination prevent women from engaging as cohesive group members, and impacts their personal lives and the well-being of operations.

1. Slut or lesbian, take your pick
Descriptive Paragraph: Participants described that part of being a woman in the Canadian Forces is to be sexualized in terms of being a slut or a whore, or a lesbian or a dyke. Participants conveyed that categorisation into these terms was established through pre-
Women Veterans of the Canadian Forces conceived reputations and assumptions. A sense was conveyed that categorisation was difficult to avoid.

Katherine: "I think that there is just always that, I think for people who came in new... I think if you are a young female corporal in a regiment and a new sergeant comes in he will think, okay well first of all I don't know anything about her. And it'll go back to the sexual bit and he will wonder if she got here because she slept with somebody or did she get here ... because she can do her job?"

2. Seen as less capable than men
Descriptive Paragraph: Participants conveyed a sense that part of the

experience of being a woman in the Canadian Forces is being seen as less capable than men. The women spoke of being compared unfavourably in terms of not being as good at their job or as capable as men.

Stephanie: "Men looked at us and thought, well you're a woman so you can't be operational. You have to be a support trade. And you had to fight; you had to continually fight to be recognized as an operational trade. And it was [a] continual battle for all the time I was it to be recognized as a woman and as in operations."

3. Proving I'm good enough
Descriptive Paragraph: Participants expressed that part of being a woman in the Canadian Forces is to have to prove you are good enough and have a right to be there. The women acknowledged a range of experiences of having to prove themselves, including working twice as hard to receive half the recognition men got or having to prove and re-prove their worth.

Andrea: "So you have to be twice as good. It was always my thought that being standard, or being like everyone else, wasn"t good enough. You had to be better and you could never be off."

4. Trying to be treated better
Descriptive Paragraph: Participants described that part of being a woman in the Canadian Forces is to strategically do things to change the way they were treated and seen, in the hope that they would be treated better. In order to do this, women used tactics such as becoming more gender-neutral or masculine in characteristics or appearances, or emphasising feminine characteristics that garner favourable treatment by men, or directly opposing the poor treatment.

Susan: "I had a shaved head then....,,cause I wanted to be a soldier.... You know, why differentiate myself, you know? I mean, we [the male soldiers and I] used to make fun of the women that differentiated themselves. I was eliminating my identification as a female ... and creating my identification as a soldier."

5. Treated like dirt
Descriptive Paragraph: Participants described that part of being a woman in the Canadian Forces is to be treated with ill will and malevolence. The participants" experiences of feeling ill will and malevolence towards them ranged from situations where men turned on them with hostility, to being physically assaulted, intentionally hurt, unprotected in a hostile environment, and treated like dirt.

Theresa: "Like I had a guy ... [and] he told anybody that knew him, and they told me after that he just, because I was lesbian, that he didn't like me. And he was, „Going to put the fucking dyke in her place". And I didn't know that when he first came to the ship. And I tried to approach him like a harassment advisor. So I said to him one day, I said, „I would like to talk to you like an adult. Because I can"t work with you the way that you treat me, like I'm dirt. I'm just not going to put up with that." And he just looked me right in the face and he said, „So do fucking something about it."

8. Perpetual outsider
Descriptive Paragraph: Participants described that part of being a woman in the Canadian Forces is to be an outsider and be separate from the group. The women described a sense of isolation, being alone, or being on the outside.

Susan: "You"re always on the outside. You always are as a woman. There were key members that you could feel true camaraderie with, but as a whole, I think, you"re always kind of on the outside..."

1. Barriers around every corner
Descriptive Paragraph: Five of the six participants described that part of their experience of being a woman in the Canadian Forces is to experience barriers and limitations to opportunities.

Nadine: "And the two officers in charge, the captain was the OC of the company and his 2IC were fairly gung ho, kind of uber-soldier guys. And they take all the women aside on the first day, I can't remember how many women initially on the first day that there were, but they quietly took us all off to the side and said, "None of you women will pass this course. Period. You won't. No woman will pass my course. So don't fool yourselves into thinking that you will."

3. That's enough! I quit!
Descriptive Paragraph: Five out of six participants described how part of being a woman in the Canadian Forces is to leave your career partially based on the mistreatment and gender discrimination encountered. Some women described an isolated incident, such as being in an overly sexually charged atmosphere, or being in an inappropriately and discriminatorily charged environment, as the tipping point where they decided they had had enough and wanted to retire. Others described a gradual process where they realized they would never be accepted and were tired of fighting for equality and instead decided to leave.

Andrea: "I left... [when] I still had a promising career. I could've had 18 years left. I was promoted faster than anyone else in the occupation. I had set records. And I knew, at a certain level, that I"d never become the top chief warrant officer because they are not ready for women.... So as a female NCO, there was no way I was going to advance. You just get knives stabbed in the back the whole time."

Appendix 2c [Sexual misconduct by Canadian Forces General]

Forces Afghan commander pleads guilty at court martial
By Juliet O'Neill, Canwest News Service, Postmedia News, May 25, 2010

GATINEAU, Que. — Brig.-Gen. Daniel Menard, the commander of Canadian Forces in Afghanistan, was fined $3,500 after pleading guilty at a court martial Tuesday to neglect in handling his C8 rifle.

A fine of $3,500, proposed for sentencing by prosecution and defense lawyers in a joint submission, was accepted by judge Mario Dutil.

The charge of neglect causing prejudice to "good order and discipline" stemmed from a March 25th incident in which Menard's personal weapon discharged twice as he prepared to leave Kandahar airfield on a Blackhawk helicopter accompanied by chief of defense staff Gen. Walt Natynczyk.

A statement of circumstances said Menard's rifle was on automatic, rather than safe, when he was preparing to depart and court heard that it fired within range of ten personnel near two armoured vehicles.

Nobody was injured and Menard immediately asked for an investigation and told his troops about the incident — factors that should mitigate the sentence, prosecuting lawyer Lt-Col. Marylene Trudel told the court.

Defense lawyer Lt-Col. Troy Sweet said Menard was a highly decorated commander with an unblemished record during a exemplary military career and he had "accepted full responsibility" right away.

Appendix 2d [Sexual misconduct by Canadian Forces Colonel]

Canada's Top Soldier in Haiti Stripped of Command
By Arthur Weinreb
Last Updated Jul 12, 2010, Published Jul 10, 2010

Col. Bernard Ouellette's removal was just the latest in a series of allegations of crime and impropriety made against members of the Canadian Forces

On July 9, 2010, the Canadian Forces announced that Col. Bernard Ouellette, the chief of staff of the UN mission in Port-au-Prince and the commander of Canada's 10 person military contingent in Haiti was relieved of his command. The reason for relieving Ouellette of his duties was an allegation that he had an improper personal relationship with a female civilian employee at the United Nations headquarters in Port-au-Prince. A military spokesperson stated that as a result of the allegations, the chain of command had lost confidence in Ouellette being able to properly carry out his mission. The spokesperson also added that both Ouellette and the unnamed woman deny the allegations that they had a relationship.

The decision was actually made on June 26, 2010 but was not made public until a journalist in Haiti began to ask questions about why Ouellette was missing. The decision had been communicated to Ouellette while he was vacationing in Quebec in June. Liberal Defense critic, Ujjal Doshanjh pointed out that since Haiti was not a war zone there was no reason to keep the firing of Ouellette a secret.

The colonel had been in Haiti since July 2009 and was due to leave this month. When the earthquake struck on January 12, 2010, Ouellette and his team were credited with rescuing UN staffers who were buried under the rubble of the mission..

Appendix 3 [What 'moron' sent our Canadian Troops to a desert campaign in bright green camouflage?]

Couldn't help think of this person's quote:
"Shit rises to the top, idiocy flourishes, and the most ridiculous policies are enacted by people without the brains to think a day into the future."

Reference to:
What Happened to Canada's Armed Forces?
Visiting Afghanistan in Green Camouflage and Returning in Black Bodybags

Everywhere you go today, in and out of the Armed Forces, you hear 'what happened to the military?' They cannot get recruits, their equipment is out dated, and they're over extended. The very infrastructure is crumbling for want of funding, etc.

Our troops were deployed to Afghanistan with 'Jolly Green Giant' new Combat uniforms while the old style khaki combat uniforms sat on the shelf. In order to survive, the soldiers had to paint their green uniforms khaki!

Jack C. Downey CD
What Happened to Canada's Armed Forces?
www.canadianculture.com/geezer/jack83.html

Reference to:
Canadians were sent Afghanistan wearing "Green" camouflage! Which sort of had the added bonus of making them just a little conspicuous.

Reference to:
Still wearing his green battle fatigues, his army boots caked in mud, Frank talked about the grief he felt when he learned his long-time friend had been killed.
Friends made a solemn pact
Nick Pron - Apr. 21, 2002

"The 24-year-old native of Barrie, Ont., was one of five "escorts" who flew home from Afghanistan with the bodies of their four fallen comrades, Pte. Smith, 27, and Pte. Richard Green, 22, Cpl. Ainsworth Dyer, 25, and Sgt. Marc Leger, 29.

The bodies and five escorts - Frank, Pte. Simon Hughes, Cpl. Kent Schmidt and Jan Rube, and Sgt. Ken Dunn - arrived at CFB Trenton yesterday morning aboard a gunmetal-gray Canadian Forces Airbus.

Following a ceremony at the base, the funeral cortege - four hearses, two limousines and a military police car - travelled to Toronto where they were joined by five Toronto police cruisers for the trip up Bay St. to the coroner's building on Grosvenor St.

Frank said everyone in Smith's platoon knew of the pact between the two friends, and afterwards they asked him to "bring him home."

Still wearing his green battle fatigues, his army boots caked in mud, Frank talked about the grief he felt when he learned his long-time friend had been killed. The two friends had been making plans to finish off the basement of Frank's home, north of Toronto, and then fill it with memorabilia from their military experiences.

Frank smiled briefly when he explained that although he and his friend used the term wife, both were referring to each other's fiancees.

"I can't even tell you the time when I found out," he continued. "It was like one in the morning Zulu time. When I found out I was just sick. It made me ill. You don't know what to say. You don't know how to react."

Frank and Hughes, an escort for his friend, Green, emerged briefly from the hearses that were parked in a laneway outside the morgue, waiting their turns to drive the remains into an underground landing at the coroner's building.

Both men, wearing black armbands, expressed their thanks to all the support and sympathy they have received from fellow Canadians since their friends were killed.

"It has been really special," Frank said.

"Just excellent," added Hughes, 32. "And we appreciate it very much."

Appendix 4a [Friendly fire]

Military rejects WikiLeaks friendly fire report
CBC News
26/07/2010 11:55:06 PM

The Canadian military is rejecting a report released by WikiLeaks that suggests four Canadian soldiers who died in September 2006 in Afghanistan were killed by friendly fire from U.S. forces.

The military maintains the four soldiers died in combat with the Taliban.

"The loss of four Canadian soldiers on September 3rd, 2006, was the result of insurgent activity in the Panjwaii district of Afghanistan," the defense minister's spokesman Jay Paxton said in an email Monday evening.

"The only friendly fire incident from the time period in question occurred on September 4th, 2006, when Private Mark Anthony Graham was killed in the same district."

The friendly fire allegation occurred in a report that was among more than 91,000 documents released Sunday revealing new details about the war in Afghanistan and describing numerous accounts of brutality, corruption, extortion and kidnapping by members of the Afghan police force.

According to an incident report filed by the U.S. military unit, 205TH RCAG (Regional Corps Advisory Group), four Canadian soldiers were killed and seven others and an interpreter were wounded on Sept. 3, 2006, when a jet dropped a bomb on a building they occupied during the second day of Operation MEDUSA.

The Canadian military reported at the time that the four soldiers died in battles with Taliban forces.

The military's Maple Leaf newsletter also said on Sept. 13, 2006, that "four soldiers were killed September 3 during Operation MEDUSA, a significant combined effort between the Afghan National Security Forces, Canada and other NATO partners in the International Security Assistance Force as they fought to drive Taliban fighters from a region west of Kandahar City."

Killed were Warrant Officer Richard Nolan of Newfoundland, Warrant Officer Frank Mellish of P.E.I. and Nova Scotia, Sgt. Shane Stachnik of

Alberta and Pte. William Cushley of Ontario.

"These officers died in an ongoing effort to force Taliban insurgents from a region West of Kandahar City so that displaced villagers can return to their homes and re-establish their livelihoods without living in constant fear," then defense minister Gordon O'Connor said in the Maple Leaf story.

On Monday, Michel Drapeau, a former colonel with the Canadian Forces, said the WikiLeaks document is disturbing, because it differs from the information provided by the military at the time of the soldiers' deaths.

"There's a wide discrepancy, and we need to know," Drapeau told As It Happens on Monday night. "One of the reports has to be accurate," he said.

The veracity of the WikiLeaks document hasn't been determined, and Drapeau acknowledged that the incident report could be wrong and not corrected.

The Canadian military says it has not been misleading about Canadian deaths.

"At all times, the Canadian Forces have been open and forthright with the families of our fallen soldiers and the Canadian public about the circumstances relating to deaths in Afghanistan," Paxton said.

One of the soldiers' mothers said she believes the military.

"The vehicle that he was in was hit by an RPG - that's a rocket-propelled grenade - and some of the shrapnel from it hit the turret and some of the shrapnel from the turret hit him in the neck. He bled to death," Avril Stachnik told The Canadian Press in an interview in Waskatenau, Alta.

"One of Shane's best friends was with him at the time and that's what he told me as well," she said.

The U.S. Pentagon would not comment on the leaked documents, including the friendly fire report.

Appendix 4b [He had, in fact, been poisoned]

The author should note, he used to see this poor guy when he lived in Peterborough.

Article: Reward for gallantry; Canadian soldiers receive a slap on the wrist for seriously poisoning an overzealous officer.
Article from: The Report Newsmagazine Article date: September 10, 2001 Author: Schuster, Eli

Before he served as a Canadian Forces peacekeeper in Croatia in 1993, Matt Stopford had a common-law wife and two children; today, the former warrant officer lives alone on a full army pension. Days go by when he cannot find the energy even to lift himself out of bed. He is losing his teeth, and a bowel disorder causes anal bleeding. At times, his one good eye throbs so painfully he must lie down in a darkened room, inject himself with cortisone and hope the retina does not explode as his other one did.

After years of telling Mr. Stopford it was not to blame for his illness, the Defense Department released a letter last year claiming he had, in fact, been poisoned …

Appendix 4c [Cowardly crime]

This cowardly crime also in:

Matt Stopford: DND still on his case
Esprit de Corps, Dec, 2003 by Bill Beswetherick

Ten years ago, PPCLI Warrant Officer Matt Stopford commanded an infantry platoon in Croatia during the most intense fighting experienced by Canadian soldiers since the Korean War. He now lives in Peterborough, is blind in one eye, suffers many ailments he claims resulted from military service, and has been given a life expectancy of ten years. Stopford, 41, is suing the Canadian Forces over its alleged failure to treat his ailments and its alleged refusal to inform him that some of his soldiers attempted to poison him. Lawyers representing the military are attempting to bar him from using the courts by claiming that because he is in receipt of a disability pension he cannot seek additional compensation. They also argue he cannot sue because the military is not contractually bound to its members.

"COWARDLY AND DESPICABLE"

In May 2000, following an investigation which included participation by the RCMP, the military announced that six of Stopford's soldiers had tried to poison him. The senior investigator stated: that "This is a case we can prove beyond a reasonable doubt"; yet, no one was disciplined. Incredibly, and despite evidence to the contrary, Chief of the Defense Staff General Ray Henault argued "there was not enough evidence to justify the extreme step of depriving any individual of their employment."

The soldiers accused claimed they only wanted to temporarily incapacitate Stopford because they claimed he was endangering their lives while trying to complete their mission, which was to protect unarmed civilians from a massacre. The Ottawa Citizen called their actions "cowardly and despicable" and noted that many other soldiers faced the same risks but did not attempt to shirk their duties by injuring or incapacitating their commander. Despite the intense fighting, no Canadian soldier was killed and only a few were lightly wounded.

DND REFUSES TO ACT DESPITE EVIDENCE

In addition to failing to take disciplinary action against the soldiers, DND also refused to reveal their names and what, if any, administrative action it might have taken against them, claiming their privacy had to be protected. It is likely that some of these soldiers now occupy leadership positions and will expect subordinates to give them the loyalty they refused Stopford.

Appendix 5a [748 Communications Unit]

National Defence Défense nationale

PROTECTED B

Canadian Forces Recruiting Centre
Detachment Victoria
827 Fort Street, Main Floor
Victoria BC V8W 1H6

F63 233 858 (DVA)

15 December 2005

Commanding Officer
748 Communications Squadron
Nanaimo Military Camp
Nanaimo BC V9R 5J9

APPLICANT FOR ENROLMENT INTO THE CF
PRIMARY RESERVE – F63 233 858   MOSID 00329

1.(PB) This applicant has been assessed as "Suitable", and is hereby recommended for enrolment into the CF Primary Reserve, in the following military occupation: R215 Sig Op.

2.(U) This recommendation for enrolment does not extend to any MOC other than those identified above, and such enrolment could be construed as grounds for the release of the enrolee, under QR&O 15.01, Item 5(e), "irregular enrolment". Authority for enrolment in any other MOC must be obtained through request to this CFRC. It may be granted with the recommendation as to the applicant's "suitability", by a CFRC Military Career Counsellor or a qualified Personnel Selection Officer, subject to the applicant meeting the required medical and education levels. The file is enclosed for your action.

3.(U) You are to complete forms CF444, DND 1707 and CF 92 in blue ink and return a copy of the CF444, CF 92 and the completed CF Self Identification Survey to this unit upon enrolment. Once the required forms are received at this office the Medical Documents will be forwarded to you. If the applicant is not enrolled, the applicant's file is to be returned with a note advising why the enrolment was not completed. This CFRC will close the file and advise the necessary agencies.

4.(U) Any questions may be directed to MCpl Marvin, 363-3904.

C.J. O'Keefe
Lieutenant (Navy)
Detachment Commander

Appendix 5b [Keep processing - 748 Communications Unit]

Nanaimo Military Camp
GD Stn A
Nanaimo, BC V9R 7B1

5671-1 (Sqn Recruiter)

17 Feb 05

CFRC Processing
827 Fort St. Victoria, BC
V8W 1H6

REFERRAL

1.   748 Communication Squadron has a position as a Signal Operator R215 available for this recruit.

2.   Request you continue processing this recruits application file.

D.R. Bowhey
Capt
Adjt
748 Comm Sqn

Appendix 6 [Good References]

REFERENCE INFORMATION

Name: _____

Title/Position: _Chair, Dept of First Nations Studies, Vancouver Island University_

Business or Personal Address: _900 Fifth St_

Nanaimo, BC. V9R 5S5

Telephone Number (day/evening): _____

Dates of Employment/Instruction: _2003 - 2007_

Applicant's Job Title/Duties: _Student_

_____

_____

Signature: _____   Date: _10 June 2008_

BACKGROUND INFORMATION

1. How well do you know the applicant? (check one)
   ( ) not well   ( ) slightly   (✓) moderately   ( ) well   ( ) very well

2. How long have you known the applicant? (check one)
   ( ) under 1 month   ( ) 1 - 6 months   ( ) 6 months to 1 year
   ( ) 1 - 3 years   (✓) 3 - 6 years   ( ) 6 - 10 years
   ( ) over 10 years

3. I am the applicant's: (check all that are applicable)
   ( ) employer   ( ) academic counsellor
   ( ) supervisor   (✓) teacher
   ( ) co-worker   ( ) friend
   ( ) principal or vice-principal ( ) a friend of the family
   ( ) school coach   ( ) clergy
   ( ) coach (outside of school)   ( ) other (describe): _____

2/8

130

Integrity: Adherence to the values of honesty and trustworthiness and the ability to resist temptations of an unethical or illegal nature.

Percentile Rating: 90

No evidence of plagiarism or cheating of any sort

Leadership: The ability to take charge, establish priorities and provide a clear sense of direction and purpose. The willingness to accept responsibility for outcomes. The ability to facilitate the accomplishment of goals by motivating others and setting a high personal standard. The ability to keep others informed and provide advice or counselling as required. The willingness to delegate appropriately and empower subordinates.

Percentile Rating: 50

Patricia is very reserved

Management Control: The ability to produce detailed, clearly defined, short- and long-term plans. The ability to coordinate and monitor the execution of tasks/projects, including the scheduling of human, material and financial resources to ensure that key objectives are met.

Percentile Rating: 80

Projects always submitted promptly

4/6

131

Analytical Skills: The ability to thoroughly assess a situation, seeking all possible relevant information and critically analyzing the issue from different perspectives. The ability to do simple calculations with numbers in a business context.

Percentile Rating: ___50___

Decision Making: The ability to make rational, realistic and sound decisions based on consideration of all the available facts and alternatives. The willingness and ability to make firm and timely decisions and commit to definite courses of actions, even when faced with limited information.

Percentile Rating: ___N/D___

Personal Impact: The ability to project a good first impression, to command attention and respect, and to show an air of self-confidence without being arrogant. Having confidence in one's own abilities and judgement, while understanding one's own limitations.

Percentile Rating: ___60___
___Confident but shy___

5/8

132

Interpersonal Skills/Tolerance: The ability to effectively and respectfully interact with individuals of different backgrounds, personalities, attitudes, opinions and values, and to show sensitivity, compassion and sincerity. The ability to be tactful yet diplomatic in dealings with others. The ability to use attending skills when interacting with others (e.g., establishing eye contact, paraphrasing, demonstrating interest, etc.).

Percentile Rating: __85__

Always respectful to peers in cross-cultural context

Conscientiousness: The ability to work hard and meet or exceed given standards. Persistently striving for excellence, even in difficult situations. Efficient, thorough, and dependable.

Percentile Rating: __75__

Always meets acceptable standards

Stress Tolerance/Self-Control: The ability to keep emotions under control when provoked or under stress, and effectively manage stress to prevent it from negatively impacting performance.

Percentile Rating: __N/D__

6/8

133

Initiative: The ability to be self-motivated and self-directed in identifying and addressing important issues. The ability to actively influence events rather than passively respond to them.

Percentile Rating: 70

Flexibility: The ability to adapt one's approach to a variety of situations. The willingness to accept innovation, change, or the non-traditional. The ability to generate new and imaginative ideas and novel solutions.

Percentile Rating: 70

Practical Intelligence: Good judgement and common sense. The ability to understand the dynamics of organizations, including formal and informal cultures and decision making processes. The ability to recognize and react to changing information, evaluate and utilize different courses of action, and react instinctively when required.

Percentile Rating: N/C

7/8

134

Oral Communications Skills: The ability to both listen and express one's ideas, feelings, questions and facts in a clear, accurate, and concise manner.

Percentile Rating: 45

Written Communications Skills: The ability to write accurately and concisely, presenting conclusions and organizing material in a clear and logical manner, using appropriate grammar, style and language.

Percentile Rating: 50

Overall Performance Assessment:

135

Appendix 7 [Clown Sized Boots Issued to Young Canadian Forces Female Member by 748 Communications Unit, Nanaimo, British Columbia, Canada]

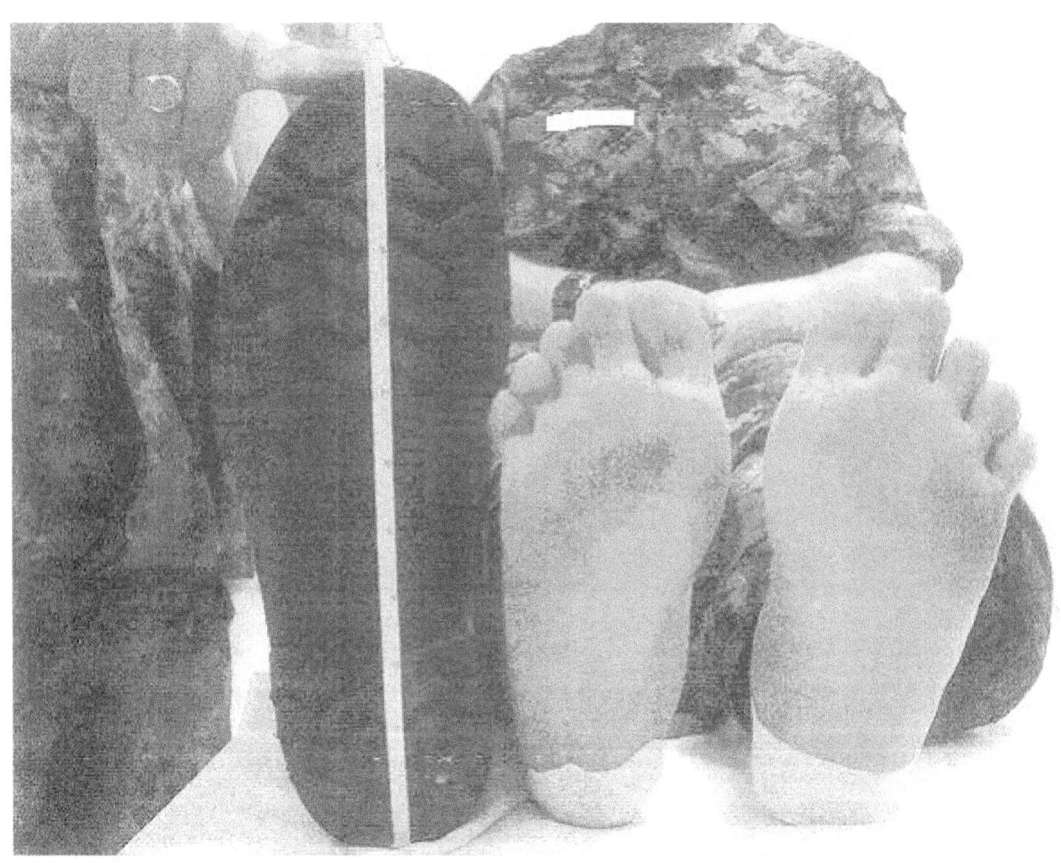

Appendix 8 [Signed Major Salsman]

DATE	UNIT UNITÉ	COMPLAINT, EXAMINATION, DIAGNOSIS, TREATMENT, DISPOSAL AND MO'S SIGNATURE / PROBLÈME, EXAMEN, DIAGNOSTIC, TRAITEMENT, ORDONNANCE ET SIGNATURE DU MÉDECIN MILITAIRE
25-4-06 8.15	CC	Blisters and hotspots on ® foot and ® foot
	HPI	Yesterday (last night) when she took her boots off, she first noticed blisters right away as well as hotspots. Pain rated 8/10.
	PPM Hx	Pt had blisters 4 mo. ago with her unit when she had even longer boots.
	Meds	Tylenol for headaches see previous entry (4 July/06)
	Allergies	Pollen + Dust
	O/E	On ® foot there is 1" long friction mark on the posterior aspect of the foot slightly proximal from the calcaneus. There is also a blister on the plantar aspect of the foot, located on the heel. It appears to be relatively deep. On the ® foot there is a similar friction mark as described on the ® foot. There are hotspots located on the bottom of both heels.
	Imp	Friction marks, hotspots and a blister caused by wearing oversized combat boots
	Plan	Enquire about new boots and dressed friction marks. Cpl Lawrence ST RCH MedTech Section. Dressed with hypafix and Mepore. Cpl Lawrence ST RCH Sect'n Should be fitted with orthotics Cpl Lawrence ST RCH Sect'n Com—
		MAJOR KR SALSMAN MO CCFT BSURO TT SFREC SHILO 15-SFS
6 Dec 06	St Jn	19 yr old ♀ c̄ FN pd ǩ bruising to ® leg. O/E blister, healing well all sign of infection

Appendix 9 [From Major Salsman]

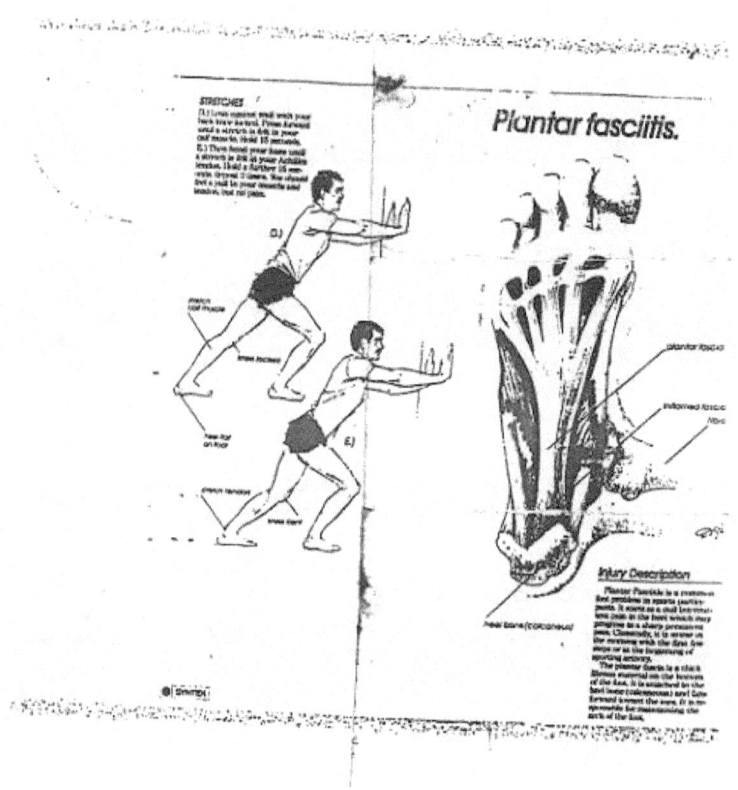

The condition usually occurs where part of this inelastic fascia is pulled away from the heel bone. This causes an inflammation and thus, pain. Plantar fasciitis injury may also occur at midsole or insole toes. Since it is difficult to rest the foot, a vicious cycle is set up with the situation aggravated with every step. In severe cases, the heel is visibly swollen. The problem worsens rapidly and treatment must be started as soon as possible.

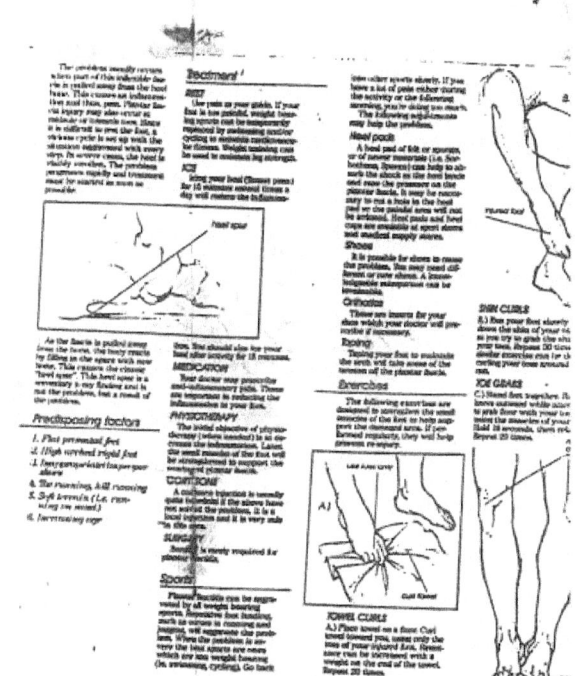

heel spur

As the fascia is pulled away from the bone, the body reacts by filling in the space with new bone. This causes the classic "heel spur". This heel spur is a secondary to any fascia and is not the problem, but a result of the problem.

Predisposing factors

1. Flat pronated feet
2. High arched rigid feet
3. Inappropriate/improper shoes
4. Too running, hill running
5. Soft terrain (i.e. running on sand)
6. Increasing age

Treatment

REST
Use pain as your guide. If your foot is too painful, weight bearing sports can be temporarily replaced by swimming another cycling to maintain cardiovascular fitness. Weight training can be used to maintain leg strength.

ICE
Icing your heel (frozen press) for 15 minutes several times a day will reduce the inflammation. You should also ice your heel after activity for 15 minutes.

MEDICATION
Your doctor may prescribe anti-inflammatory pills. These are important to reducing the inflammation in your foot.

PHYSIOTHERAPY
The initial objective of physiotherapy (when needed) is to decrease the inflammation. Later, the small muscles of the foot will be strengthened to support the weakened plantar fascia.

CORTISONE
A cortisone injection is usually quite helpful if the above have not solved the problem. It is a local injection and it is very safe in this area.

SURGERY
Surgery is rarely required for plantar fasciitis.

Sports
Plantar fasciitis can be aggravated by all weight bearing sports. Repetitive foot landing, such as occurs in running and jogging, will aggravate the problem. Where the problem is severe the best sports are ones which are non weight bearing (i.e. swimming, cycling). Go back

into other sports slowly. If you have a lot of pain either during the activity or the following morning, you're doing too much.

The following adjustments may help the problem.

Heel pads
A heel pad of felt or sponge, or of newer materials (i.e. Sorbothane, Spenco) can help to absorb the shock at the heel heels and ease the pressure on the plantar fascia. It may be necessary to cut a hole in the heel pad so the painful area will not be irritated. Heel pads and heel cups are available at sport stores and medical supply stores.

Shoes
It is possible for shoes to cause the problem. You may need different or new shoes. A knowledgeable salesperson can be invaluable.

Orthotics
These are inserts for your shoe which your doctor will prescribe if necessary.

Taping
Taping your foot to maintain the arch will take some of the tension off the plantar fascia.

Exercises
The following exercises are designed to strengthen the small muscles of the foot to help support the damaged arch. If performed regularly, they will help prevent re-injury.

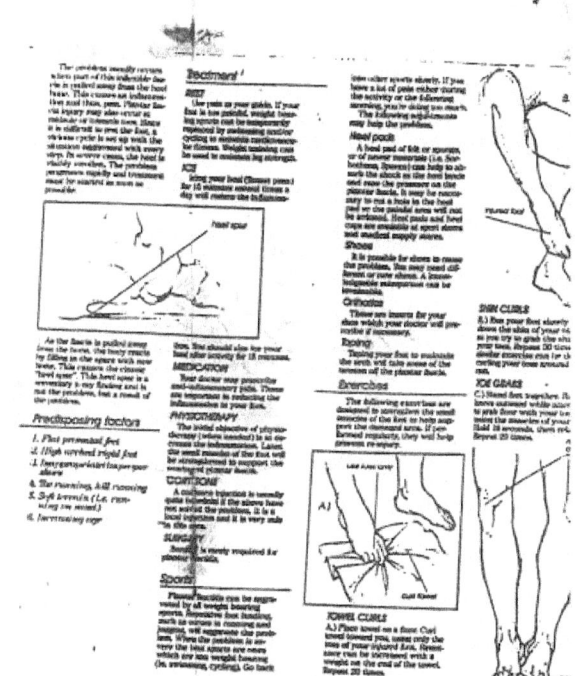

A.)

Towel Curl

TOWEL CURLS
A.) Place towel on a floor. Curl towel toward you, using only the toes of your injured foot. Resistance can be increased with a weight on the end of the towel. Repeat 20 times.

flexed foot

SHIN CURLS
B.) Run your foot slowly down the shin of your other leg as you try to grab the shin with your toes. Repeat 20 times. Similar exercise can be done curling your toes around your shin.

TOE GRASP
C.) Stand feet together. Slowly move outward while using to grab floor with your toes using the muscles of your feet. Hold 10 seconds, then relax. Repeat 20 times.

Appendix 10 [Running shoes until receives proper fitting boots]

Appendix 11 [Take it easy]

Appendix 12 [Proper boots to perform military duty - Signed Major Salsman]

18400-1 (B Surg)

10 July 06

Distr List

<u>MODIFICATIONS TO FOOTWEAR</u>

Refs: A. CFMO 6-52
B. A-LM-007-014-AG-001 Chap 3, Sect 8

1.   Please provide and fit this member with two pair of vibram-soled combat boots with adequate width and depth to accommodate her wide feet.

    a.   Name: I

    b.   Rank: Pte.;

    c.   SN: Unit: 3 Squad BMQ; and

    d.   Tel: I

2.   I have determined that this item is reqr in the performance of this members military duty.

3.   IAW the refs, req you proceed with procurement of this item.

K.R. Salsman
Maj
B Surg
3150

Distr List

B Sup O
Med Rcds (CF2034)

Appendix 13 [Infected foot - toe]

Appendix 14 [Infected foot]

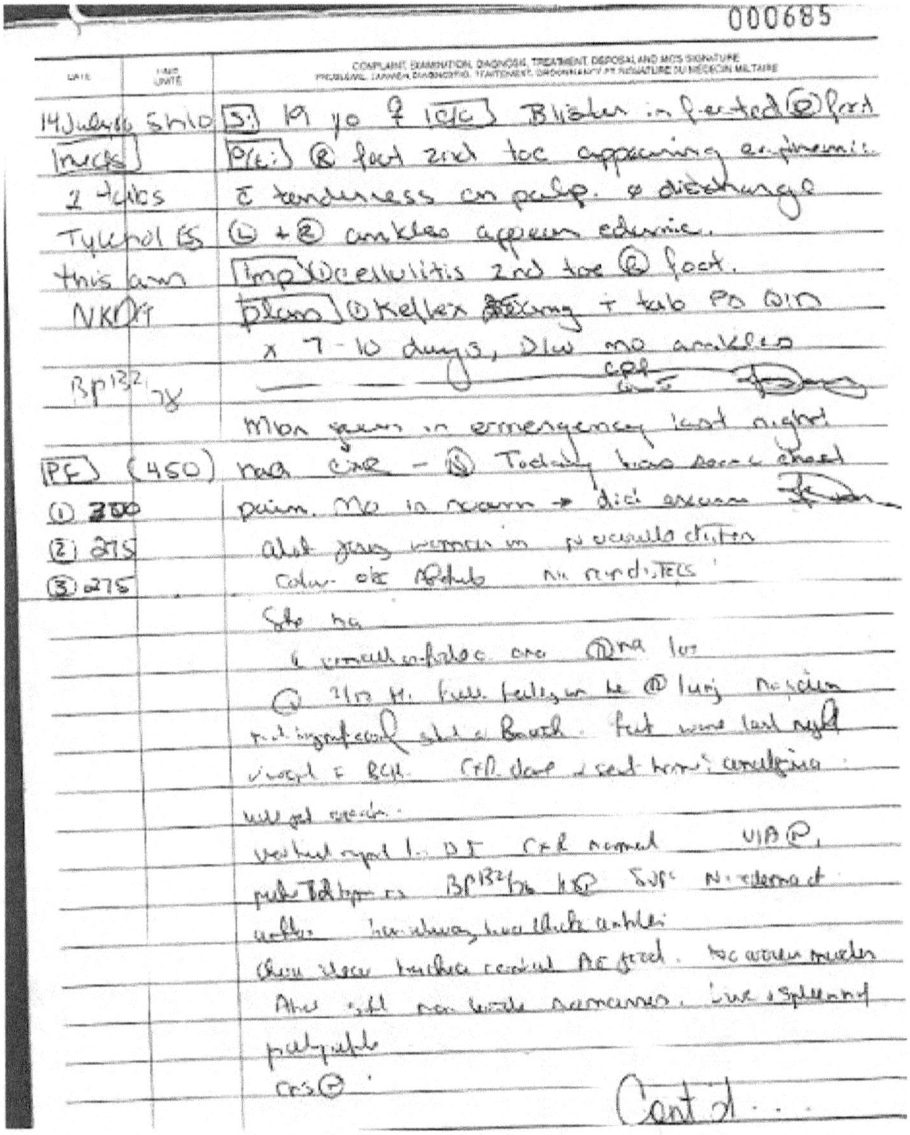

000685

DATE	UNIT / UNITÉ	COMPLAINT, EXAMINATION, DIAGNOSIS, TREATMENT, DISPOSAL AND MO'S SIGNATURE / PROBLÈME, EXAMEN, DIAGNOSTIC, TRAITEMENT, ORDONNANCE ET SIGNATURE DU MÉDECIN MILITAIRE
14 July 06	5 Wg	S:) 19 yo ♀ [illegible] Blister infected (R) foot
Meds)		PE:) (R) foot 2nd toe appearing erythematous
2 tabs		c̄ tenderness on palp. ø discharge
Tylenol ES		(L) + (R) ankles appear edematous.
this am		Imp) (1) cellulitis 2nd toe (R) foot.
NKDA		plan) (1) Keflex [illegible] ī tab PO QID
		x 7-10 days, D/W MO ankles
BP 132/78		
		MO [illegible] in emergency last night
PF) (450)		had CXR – (N) Today has some chest
(1) 300		pain. MO in room → did exam
(2) 275		[illegible]
(3) 275		[illegible]
		[illegible]
		[illegible]
		[illegible]
		[illegible]
		[illegible]
		[illegible] CXR normal [illegible]
		[illegible] BP 132/[illegible] [illegible]
		[illegible]
		[illegible]
		[illegible]
		palpable
		CVS (N)
		Cont'd . . .

Appendix 15 [Antibiotic for infected foot]

Base Medical Clinic
CF3 Shilo
Shilo, MB R0K 2A0 CANADA
Phone: (204) 765-3000   Fax: (204) 765-3303

This Counselling Information was printed for
Rx Number 50359
APO-CEPHALEX 250 MG   DIN: 00768723   Pharm: MP

IMPORTANT NOTE: The following information is intended to supplement, not substitute for, the expertise and judgment of your physician, pharmacist or other healthcare professional. It should not be construed to indicate that use of the drug is safe, appropriate, or effective for you. Consult your healthcare professional before using this drug.

CEPHALEXIN - ORAL (sef-a-LEX-in)

COMMON BRAND NAME(S): Keflex

USES: This medication is a cephalosporin-type antibiotic used to treat a wide variety of bacterial infections (e.g., skin, bone and genitourinary tract infections).

OTHER USES: This drug may also be used before dental procedures in patients with artificial heart valves to prevent serious infection of the heart lining (bacterial endocarditis).

HOW TO USE: Take this medication by mouth usually every 6 or 12 hours, or as directed by your doctor. You may take this medicine with food if stomach upset occurs.
   Antibiotics work best when the amount of medicine in your body is kept at a constant level. Therefore, take this drug at evenly spaced intervals.
   Continue to take this medication until the full-prescribed amount is finished even if symptoms disappear after a few days. Stopping this medication too early may allow bacteria to continue to grow, which may result in a relapse of the infection.
   Inform your doctor if your condition persists or worsens.

SIDE EFFECTS: Stomach upset, headache, fatigue, dizziness, or diarrhea may occur. If any of these effects persist or worsen, notify your doctor or pharmacist promptly.
   Tell your doctor immediately if any of these unlikely but serious side effects occur: mental/mood changes.
   Tell your doctor immediately if any of these highly unlikely but very serious side effects occur: stomach/abdominal pain, persistent nausea/vomiting, yellowing eyes or skin, dark urine, new signs of infection (e.g., persistent sore throat or fever), easy bruising/bleeding, change in the amount of urine.
   This medication may rarely cause a severe intestinal condition (pseudomembranous colitis) due to a resistant bacteria. This condition may occur while receiving therapy or even weeks after treatment has stopped. Do not use anti-diarrhea products or narcotic pain medications if you have the following symptoms because such products may make them worse. Tell your doctor immediately if you develop persistent diarrhea, abdominal or stomach pain/cramping, or blood/mucus in your

---

Formation Health Services
Our Pharmacists will be pleased to answer any questions

Page 1
724-0114 / 334

Printed on 7/14/2006

145

Appendix 16 [Recommend Medical RTU]

Date: _____ Service #: _____

Rank: _____ Name: _____

Local Unit: _____ Course: _____

Time In: _____ Time Out: _____

_____ No Drill
_____ No Marching
_____ Unfit Parades
_____ No Running
_____ No Walking more than _____
_____ No PT
_____ PT at own Pace
_____ No Upper Body PT
_____ No Lower Body PT
_____ Wear Running Shoes
_____ No Ruck or Webbing Marches
_____ No Lifting more than _____
_____ No Unarmed Combat or Pugil Stick Fighting
_____ Unfit Field
_____ Unfit Rangers
_____ Unfit Weapons Handling
_____ Physio Directed Activity Only
_____ All activities at own pace
_____ Minimal use of _____
_____ No Prolonged Standing
_____ Desk Work Only
_____ Sedentary Work Only
_____ May Attempt Course Requirements

Other Instructions: Recheck _____

Recommend medical RTU

M&D   Light Duties X _____
Sick in Quarters _____   Meals brought to member
Bed Rest _____   Y   N
Excused Duties _____
Signature: _____

M&D:	No Restrictions
Light Duties:	Members activities limited as indicated above
Sick in Quarters:	Must remain in quarters but may move about freely. Activities as tolerated.
Bed Rest:	Must remain in bed. May get up to use washroom and go to meals only. (unless otherwise indicated above)
Excused Duties:	Member is excused from duties and is free to move about base. Activities as tolerated.

Appendix 17 [Recommend Medical RTU]

A medical form with the following fields:

Date: _____ Service #: _____
Rank: Pte _____ Name: _____
Home Unit: _____ Course: BMQ _____
Time In: 15:15 Time Out: 1550

Checklist items:
- No Drill
- No Marching
- Unfit Parades
- No Running
- No Walking more than _____
- No PT
- PT at own Pace
- No Upper Body PT
- No Lower Body PT
- Wear Running Shoes
- No Ruck or Webbing Marches
- No Lifting more than _____
- No Unarmed Combat or Pugil Stick Fighting
- Unfit Field
- Unfit Rangers
- Unfit Weapons Handling
- Physio Directed Activity Only
- ✓ All activities at own pace
- Minimal use of _____
- No Prolonged Standing
- Desk Work Only
- Sedentary Work Only
- May Attempt Course Requirements

Other Instructions: _____ Recheck _____

Recommend medical RTU as a musculoskeletal today

M&D
Sick in Quarters: _____ Light Duties X _____ Meals brought to member Y N
Bed Rest: _____
Excused Duties: _____
Signature: _____

M&D: No Restrictions
Light Duties: Members activities limited as indicated above.
Sick in Quarters: Must remain in quarters but may move about freely. Activities as tolerated.
Bed Rest: Must remain in bed. May get up to use washroom and go to meals only. (unless otherwise indicated above)
Excused Duties: Member is excused from duties and is free to move about base. Activities as tolerated.

147

Appendix 18 [Recommend Medical RTU – Medical Base Surgeon who is Major Salsman]

COURSE REPORT

NOTE: INSTRUCTIONS FOR PREPARATION AND DISTRIBUTION ARE CONTAINED IN CFAO 26-12

National Defense
Défense Nationale

PROTECTED B
SECURITY CLASSIFICATION - COTE DE SÉCU.

RAPPORT DE COURS

NOTA: LES INSTRUCTIONS RELATIVES À LA RÉDACTION ET À LA DIFFUSION DU PRÉSENT DOCUMENT SE TROUVENT DANS L'OAFC 26-12

PERSONNAL DATA- RENSEIGNEMENTS PERSONNELS

2. RANK - GRADE: Pte R

3. SURNAME - NOM DE FAMILLE

4. MOC - GPM: R215

5. PARENT UNIT - UNITÉ D'APPARTENANCE

6. FIRST OFFICIAL LANGUAGE - PREMIÈRE LANGUE OFFICIELLE
English/Anglais [X] 1, French/Français [ ] 2, Other/Autre [ ]

12. DISPOSITION - DISPOSITIONS

COURSE DATA - RENSEIGNEMENTS SUR LE COURS

7. COURSE TITLE - TITRE DU COURS: Basic Military Qualification

8. COURSE CODE - N° DE CODE DU COURS: 103673

9. TRAINING DAYS - JOURS D'INSTRUCTION: Scheduled 24, Required 24

10. COURSE DATES - DATES DU COURS: From 03 Jul 06 To 01 Aug 06

11. COURSE SER NO. - N° DE SÉRIE DU COURS: 0179

13. LANGUAGE OF INSTRUCTION - LANGUE D'INSTRUCTION
English/Anglais [X] 1, French/Français [ ] 2

16. PHYSICAL FITNESS TEST - EXAMEN D'APTITUDE PHYSIQUE

17. GENERAL COMMENTS - REMARQUES GÉNÉRALES

The DP1 Basic Military Qualification (BMQ) was conducted in accordance with the Course Training Plan A-PD-050-BMQ/PH-H16 dated May 2003 which is based upon the Canadian Forces Non-Commissioned Members General Specification (NCMGS) as published in A-PD-055-002/PP-002. The aim of the training and education resulting from the BMQ TP is to provide the individual with the basic common core skills and knowledge necessary to perform their duties required of all members of the military.

BMQ - Qualification Code AIOY

Pte _____ passed the following:
PO 101 Apply GMK (00%);
PO 105 St John Ambulance Standard First Aid Training, and Cardio-Pulmonary Resuscitation (Adult) Training on 11 July 06 (91%); and
Standard for Harassment Awareness and Racism Prevention Training on 07 July 06.

Pte _____ failed written test on PO 109 Maintain Safe Working Environment (50%).

On 14 July, the Base Surgeon recommended Pte _____ for medical RTU.

Immediately following the PRB convened on 17 July Pte _____, was removed from training that same day, having completed 11 days of training.

18. STUDENT - STAGIAIRE
Date: 17 Jul 06

19. REPORTING OFFICER - OFFICIER RAPPORTEUR
Date: 17 Jul 06
Signature: W. Denny MWO

20. COMMENTS BY REVIEWING OFFICER - REMARQUES DE L'OFFICIER RÉVISEUR DU RAPPORT

Pte _____ passed PO 101, and 105 in the BMQ without difficulty however failed PO 109. Pte _____ experienced difficult obtaining the inspection standard in comparison to her peers. She put a very good effort to improve her physical fitness level. Pte _____ displayed good academics and with added confidence I believe Pte _____ can succeed.

148

Appendix 19 [I don't know anything – ha, ha!]

11 Canadian Forces Health Services Centre
PO Box 5000 Station Main
Canadian Forces Base Shilo
Shilo MB R0K 2A0

6640-1 (B Surg)

17 July 2006

Adjutant
Communication Reserve School
PO Box 5000 Station Main
Canadian Forces Base Shilo
Shilo MB R0K 2A0

MEDICAL STATUS
PRIVATE [

1.　I have been asked to provide medical input into this patient's condition and use of medical services while on course here. One Medical Officer followed her until he asked me to review her case because he could not find anything wrong.

2.　Private　　　, arrived in Shilo on the long weekend in July 2006 and first reported to the MIR on 04 July 2006. There were almost daily (seven visits in 10 days with one weekend) visits for a variety of vague yet disturbing physical complaints. None of which we could find a cause for and mysteriously went away. At one point she asked to stay over night (we have no holding capability). During the stretch of numerous visits she even went to the local Emergency Department. No diagnosis was found then either. Once weekend sick parade started she came to that as well. On the day she did not come, she called the duty medical team to report nefarious symptoms. She was seen again that Monday and still all of her tests were negative as was her exam.

3.　I am unsure what is wrong with this lady but I suspect she needs to return to unit and I am quite sure she is unable to tolerate a military environment. She has easily spent more time in my clinic then on her course

4.　If further information is required, please do not hesitate to contact the undersigned at local 3150.

K.R Salsman
Major
Base Surgeon

Appendix 20 [Missed primary BMQ requirements due to "clown sized boots" issued by 748 Comm Unit and infected foot]

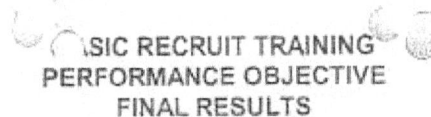

SIC RECRUIT TRAINING
PERFORMANCE OBJECTIVE
FINAL RESULTS

SN: _ _ _ _ _ _   NAME:

DP 1 - BASIC MILITARY QUALIFICATION	P/F
PO 101 – Apply General Military Knowledge	P
PO 102 – Operate the Service Rifle	DNC
PO 103 – Maintain Physical Fitness Proficiency	N/A
PO 104 – Perform Drills	DNC
PO 105 – Administer First Aid	P
PO 106 – Field Training	DNC
PO 107 – Survive Under NBC Conditions	DNC
PO 108 – Communicate Orally and In Writing	N/A
PO 109 – Maintain a Safe Working Environment	F
EDO 101 – Identify Professional Development Concepts Affecting Military Personnel	P
EDO 102 – Leadership in Peace and War	P
DNC: Did Not Complete P: Pass F: Fail	DNC

Appendix 21 [Plantar fasciitis]

Dr. Richard C. Pistone Podiatric Corporation

FOOT CARE FOR   201-1808 BOWEN ROAD, NANAIMO, B.C. V9S 5W4   Ph: (250) 754-4192   Fax: (250) 754-771
INFANTS
CHILDREN
ADULTS

February 22, 2007

To Whom It May Concern,

Re:

  I

This 20 year old female presented herself to my office February 14, 2007, complaining of
recent plantar foot pain.   had no pain in her feet at the time of the appointment.
When her feet were palpated at the insertion of the plantar fascia,   said that is
where the pain was. I   has been wearing orthotics made by a Certified Orthotist for
this past month, and today she is asymptomatic.

My examination revealed this patient has bilateral pes planus feet with a very low angle
of inclination of the calcaneii, in addition to posterior tibial dysfunction level I.

A high top lace type shoe often does help this condition because the high top holds the
ankle over the foot. Vibram soles are meaningless, either way. Orthotics with moderate
cast fill should help. I   has pes planus feet that are part of her gene pool. Shoes
can not cause this condition. Some shoes as well as the correct orthotics can help this
condition, but can not change the pes planus foot.

Sincerely,

Richard C. Pistone, D.P.M.

RCP:cm

Appendix 22 [Simple orthotics solved the problem]

OrthotiCare Clinics Inc.
Sports and Orthopaedic Bracing

#26   1700 Bowen Road
Nanaimo, B.C. V9S 1G9
Ph. (250) 753-0315
In Pinetree Mall

Patient

Diagnosis: bil. plantar fasciitis/pes planus

R

bil. custom
foot orthoses

Dr.

Date   5 Jan/07.

Appendix 23 [General W.Z. Natynczyk's letter dated 29 January, 2010]

PROTECTED B

Copy for
D.E.O.
application
w/o Recruiting

Chief of the Defence Staff

Chef d'état-major de la Défense

National Defence
Headquarters
Ottawa, Ontario
K1A 0K2

Quartier général de
la Défense nationale
Ottawa (Ontario)
K1A 0K2

(A)

5080-1-07-M-38775 (CDS)

JAN 29 2010

I have considered your grievance dated 14 December 2006, and the addendum dated 18 December 2006, concerning your objection to being released from the Canadian Forces (CF) following your return to unit (RTU) from the Basic Military Qualifications (BMQ) course at Canadian Forces Base Shilo.

Matters Grieved. In your original submission, you contend that you were never issued corrective boots as per Major (Maj) Salsman's order dated 10 July 2006, and that you were diagnosed with plantar fasciitis due to improper boots being issued by your home unit, 748 Communication Squadron (Comm Sqn), Nanaimo. You also grieve your release from the CF. In your addendum, you indicate that your home unit never measured your feet to determine the appropriate size boots for your initial issue, and that this failure denied you the opportunity to fairly participate in the BMQ. Finally, you contend that there is no telling what you might have accomplished had you been equipped with proper fitting boots.

Redress Sought. As redress, you initially requested to be reinstated in the CF, have your situation reclassified as a medical RTU, be issued the remaining monies in your summer contract, and be issued with properly fitting boots. In subsequent correspondence, you also request to be reimbursed for the cost of foot casts, payment of orthotic expenses, and compensation for pain and suffering. Finally, you request an apology.

I have reviewed your original grievance and your other comments that followed, as well as those of senior staff at this Headquarters with the responsibility for the issues you raise in your grievance. These comments have been disclosed to you. In addition, pursuant to *Queen's Regulations and Orders* (QR&O) article 7.12 (Referral to Grievance Board), your grievance was referred to the Canadian Forces Grievance Board (CFGB), which conducted an independent review of your grievance and provided findings and recommendations for my consideration, which were also disclosed to you.

1/7

National   Défense
Defence   nationale

Canada

PROTECTED B

153

The CFGB summarized the pertinent facts relating to your grievance on pages 2 to 8 of its report. I am satisfied that the summary is complete and I concur with it with the exception of one minor point. The CFGB states that the Progress Review Board (PRB) recommended that a thorough medical assessment be carried out at your home unit to determine whether you were able to meet the BMQ requisites. This is not an entirely accurate summary of the PRB recommendations. Rather, the PRB recommended that a Career Review Board be held to determine your ability to complete the BMQ course and that you undergo further medical evaluations prior to being considered for a future BMQ course.[1] Notwithstanding this minor inaccuracy, it is noted that the CFGB does rely on factual evidence in its analysis.

The CFGB's review and report with respect to the positions of the parties is set out in pages 8 to 12 of its report. These sections capture your position on these matters, as I understand it, and that of the CF authorities in respect of your grievance. I am satisfied that this report is complete and I concur with it.

Subsequent to reviewing the CFGB findings and recommendations, additional research regarding the size of footwear you were issued was conducted. The documentary results of this research were disclosed to you on 30 June 2009. I note that you have not provided any additional comments. I am now satisfied that all information pertinent to the matters you raise has been thoroughly considered.

The CFGB analyzed each of the contentions raised in your grievance file and found that the Commander Communication Reserve (Comd Comm Res), having been involved in a review of the file concerning your release, should not have acted as initial authority (IA) for your grievance. I do not agree. I find that the decision to support the Commanding Officer's (CO) recommendation to issue a Notice of Intent to Release was signed by Lieutenant-Colonel Hoekstra, Communication Reserve Chief of Staff.[2] Further, the release authority was your CO and not Comd Comm Res. Therefore, Colonel Vertefeuille, Comd Comm Res, was the correct IA for your grievance.[3] As such, the IA was not involved in reviewing the release recommendation, and was thus able to render a decision without bias.

The CFGB found that you did not receive properly fitting combat boots prior to your BMQ course, but that prompt action was taken to rectify this situation once it was identified by medical authorities; that your unsatisfactory performance on the BMQ was not due to your foot problems; that the decision for your RTU was correctly characterized as being for reasons other than medical; that your release

(handwritten annotation: Boots NEVER issued !!)

---

[1] CFGB page 000280
[2] CFGB page 000252
[3] CFGB page 000372

2/7

154

under item 5(d) to the table to QR&O article 15.01 (Release of Officers and Non-Commissioned Members) was appropriate; that you are not entitled to any further pay or allowances, nor to the issue of boots at public expense since you are no longer a serving member; that your foot condition is congenital and not attributable to military service, hence you are not entitled to reimbursement for foot casts or orthotics; that there is no basis upon which to recommend an apology or compensation for pain, suffering and embarrassment; and that there is no evidence that you were discriminated against on the grounds of your alleged disability or your gender. I concur with these findings.

The CFGB recommended that I deny your grievance. I concur with this recommendation. My reasons are provided in the paragraphs that follow.

Analysis. *Combat Boots.* Information regarding the sizing of combat boots and the CF supply procedures detailing how sizing is to be determined were disclosed to you. You were initially issued a pair of combat boots MKIII, stock number 8430-21-872-4312,[4] that corresponds to a Mondopoint[5] size of 276 millimetre (mm) in length and 108(F) mm width. From the photo evidence provided by you, it can be seen that your foot measures approximately 216 mm in length and 105 mm in width. With a three mm thick standard military issue grey sock, the measurements increase to 218 and 108 mm. The shortest standard size combat boot that will accommodate your width requirement corresponds exactly to the boot you were issued.

Notwithstanding this, the Canadian Forces Supply Manual details the responsibility of supply officers and the procedures to be followed to ensure all personnel are issued with correctly measured and fitted footwear. This manual states that:

> Improperly fitted footwear affects the general well being of an individual, often to such an extent as to impair health, morale and efficiency. It is, therefore, of the utmost importance that individuals wear footwear for which they have been measured and properly fitted.[6]

I find that the boot fitting procedures set out in the supply manual were not followed by supply personnel at 748 Comm Sqn, Nanaimo. I further find that the issuance of improperly fitted combat boots resulted in temporary foot blisters, which I note were corrected with a mild pain reliever and antibiotics.

---

[4] CFGB page 000284
[5] Mondopoint is defined as 'the... method for designating shoe sizes. It provides that the marking should consist of two numbers: (1)... the length in millimetres (measured weight-on, wearing [socks] of the average foot, and (2)... the joint width in millimetres... of the average foot fitted.' Dyck, W. *A Study of the relationship between foot size and combat boot size in the Canadian Forces.* Defence R&D Canada Technical Report No. DCIEM TR 2000-137, December 2000.
[6] Canadian Forces Supply Manual. Chapter 13 (Clothing and Personal Equipment) section 3-13G-003 (Measuring and fitting of footwear), paragraph 12.

3/7

155

The Canadian Forces Supply Manual also provides that if an individual's foot size is not within the range of standard sizes, the individual is to be provided with locally purchased special size footwear.[7] Special size footwear includes orthopaedic footwear, which is defined as custom footwear required by individuals with deformed feet. Veterans Affairs Canada defines pes planus, the genetic condition from which you suffer, as a deformed foot.[8] As such, you qualified to be fitted for orthopaedic footwear. However, base supply sections are not responsible to initiate an order for orthopaedic footwear, rather such footwear is to be obtained through an approved orthopaedic facility following a recommendation by a medical board or specialist.[9]

The Canadian Forces Medical Orders (CFMO) detail a three-part review process for enrolment medicals.[10] The first two parts are conducted at the CF recruiting centre level, and consist of preliminaries including a history and physical examination, and the third part consists of approval of the assigned medical category conducted by the Recruiting Zone Medical Officer. There is no provision or reference to recruits who may require to be seen by a specialist officer to assess a pre-enrolment medical condition such as pes planus. You participated in your enrolment medical by completing the Report of Physical Examination form[11] in which you indicated that you did not suffer from any foot trouble.

As such, while it is regrettable that your need for special orthopaedic footwear was not identified prior to attending the BMQ, and that as a result, you suffered from uncomfortable foot blisters, I find that this situation was caused by oversight, and not negligence, since neither the 748 Comm Sqn Nanaimo supply section nor the CF medical officer at Canadian Forces Recruiting Centre Victoria could have known that orthopaedic footwear would be required. Based on this observation, I find that the earliest opportunity at which you could have been assessed as requiring orthopaedic footwear was upon examination by Maj Salsman. I find that Maj Salsman, despite not being an orthopaedic specialist,[12] acted immediately to recommend the purchase of special size boots, and that his recommendation was accepted and acted upon immediately. Thus, I conclude that once your condition was known, the CF acted responsibly to address the situation.

---

[7] Ibid. section 3-13G-003, paragraph 17.
[8] CFGB page 0000653.
[9] Canadian Forces Supply Manual, Chapter 13, section 3-13G-002 (Special size personal allotment clothing, footwear and orthopaedic furniture), paragraph 6a.
[10] CFMO 27-17 (Enrolment Medical Procedures)
[11] CFGB page 000694.
[12] CFMO 6-52 Policy for Orthopaedic Supplies CF Health Services, paragraph 79 provides that "in all cases, orthotic footwear will only be issued when it has been prescribed by a specialist physician, normally an orthopaedic surgeon or a physical medicine and rehabilitation specialist. This includes the initial issue...."

4/7

156

Performance on BMQ. The CFGB notes in its findings and recommendations that you visited the Medical Inspection Room on 11 occasions over a period of 14 days. I note that some of these visits were not self-initiated, but rather, on at least three occasions you were required to report back the next day for a medical recheck. However, I also note that on these recheck visits, you raised other health issues that were not related to your foot condition. While I can understand that having poorly fitted boots and foot blisters may have effected your morale and motivation, I find that the vagueness of your health complaints and the fact that no specific diagnosis could be found speaks more to your personal disposition. This is reflected in the Base Surgeon's letter wherein he opines that you are not able to tolerate a military environment.

By the third day of the course, you were no longer required to wear the combat boots, yet you continued to display great difficulty meeting the minimum standards for dress and deportment, kit inspections, following orders and applying knowledge outside the classroom. Overall, you were found to be struggling with the day-to-day aspects of the BMQ because you lacked the aptitude to demonstrate a proper military bearing. The opinions of the Base Surgeon and training staff are based on their personal observations and, while independently raised, they are mutually supporting. Thus, I find that your RTU for reasons other than medical was warranted.

CO Decision to Release. The policy governing Administrative Reviews for members of the Communication Reserve that was in effect at the time you were issued your Notice of Intent to Release, provides that:

> A Reserve Force member who fails BMQ shall be released from the CF under item 5(d) except if the failure is for medical/compassionate reasons. At the sole discretion of the Commanding Officer, the Commanding Officer may recommend the retention of a member who was returned to unit or failed a course for medical/compassionate reasons otherwise the Commanding Officer shall release the member.[13]

As such, whether you were RTU for medical, or other, reasons, I find that your CO had the requisite authority to initiate your release and that all proceedings regarding your release were carried out with due procedural fairness. I further find that your release was not related to your disability or gender but rather it was attributable to your personal unsuitability for service in a military environment. As such, your allegations of discrimination are unfounded.

Decision. I am satisfied that you have been treated appropriately in accordance with the regulations governing release and that there are no grounds upon which to award you any financial compensation. Consequently, I do not grant the redress that you seek.

---

[13] Communication Reserve Directive 120 (Note: Administrative Reviews are also known as Career Reviews.)

5/7

PROTECTED B

Should you disagree, you are at liberty to submit your case for financial compensation for lost wages directly to the Director – Claims and Civil Litigation at the following address:

Director – Claims and Civil Litigation
Department of National Defence and Canadian Forces Legal Advisor
10th Floor, Constitution Building
305 Rideau Street
Ottawa ON K1A 0K2

Post-Decision Details. You are hereby advised that as the Chief of the Defence Staff, I am the final authority in the CF grievance process in accordance with section 29.11 (Final Authority) of the *National Defence Act* (NDA). Pursuant to section 29.15 (Decision is final) of the NDA, "A decision of a final authority in the grievance process is final and binding and, except for judicial review under the Federal Courts Act, is not subject to appeal or to review by any court."

The provisions of the *Federal Courts Act* state in paragraph 18.1(2) (Time limitation), "An application for judicial review in respect of a decision or an order of a federal board, commission or other tribunal shall be made within 30 days after the time the decision or order was first communicated..." Should you wish to seek review of my decision, you can do so through the Federal Courts within 30 days of receipt of this letter.

For identification purposes, your service number is

Queries may be directed to the Director General Canadian Forces Grievance Authority – Enquiries and Complaints Officer at the following toll free number 1-866-474-3867.

I wish to take this opportunity to wish you well in your future endeavours.

W.J. Natynczyk
General

Distribution List (Page7)

Copy to C.H.R.C.

6/7

PROTECTED B

Appendix 24 [Bandaged heels]

Reference L of the above relates to a memo written by the 748 Comm Sqn Operations Warrant Officer (Ops WO) (pp.203-204) regarding photos (pp.156 and 744) that were e-mailed to the unit from the Comm Res School on 11 July (pp.198-202). These photos were originated by a Sergeant at the Shilo Health Services Unit on 5 July 2006 and depict the grievor's feet with bandaged heels, next to combat boots that extend several inches beyond her toes. The e-mail photos were sent under the heading "oversized boots" up the Chain of Command to the Comm Res School and to the grievor's unit.

Remember that General W.Z. Natynczyk on page 3 of his letter dated 29 January, 2010 confirmed that "I find that the boot fitting procedures set out in the supply manual were not followed by supply personnel at 748 Comm Sqn, Nanaimo" with regard to this **young Canadian Forces female member** [see Appendix 23].

Appendix 25 [Clown sized boots issued and he thought the problem had been corrected?]

In response to these e-mails, the Ops WO explained the procedures followed by the unit to issue the grievor's combat boots. Contrary to the grievor's assertion that she complained to personnel at the unit about her boots (p.486), the Ops WO indicated that the grievor had never indicated there was a problem. According to the Ops WO and the Basic Training List Non-Commissioned Officer (BTL NCO) not only had several attempts been made to ensure that the grievor's boots fit properly, he had enquired himself as he had noticed she had a tendency to drag her feet. He also indicated that he thought the problem had been corrected (p.204).

Remember that General W.Z. Natynczyk on page 3 of his letter dated 29 January, 2010 confirmed that "I find that the boot fitting procedures set out in the supply manual were not followed by supply personnel at 748 Comm Sqn, Nanaimo" with regard to this **young Canadian Forces female member** [see Appendix 23].

160

Appendix 26 [Kathryn Lavery of the Canadian Human Rights Commission accepts Canadian Forces lame comments]

PROTECTED B

National Defence   Défense nationale

26

National Defence Headquarters   Quartier général de la Défense nationale
Ottawa, Ontario   Ottawa (Ontario)
K1A 0K2   K1A 0K2

WITHOUT PREJUDICE

6557-1-   (DHRD 2-4-2)

7 July 2010

Ms. Kathryn Lavery
Early Resolution Advisor
Canadian Human Rights Commission
Suite 1845 Canada Place
9700 Jasper Avenue
Edmonton AB   T5J 4C3

Dear Ms. Lavery,

b.   "She was issued boots by her home unit in Nanaimo, British Columbia, that did not fit her." The complainant's initial kit issue was on 31 January 2006. It is important to note that senior staff at the squadron noticed that the complainant tended to drag her feet as she walked. The Operations

> Warrant Officer asked her if her boots fit properly to which she replied they did. The Operations Warrant Officer, not convinced, requested the Chief Clerk follow up to determine if her boots fit. It was at that time she first reported that they did not. The complainant was sent to Canadian Forces Base (CFB) Esquimalt on two separate occasions, 17 and 22 February 2006, to correct her kit deficiencies (specifically improper fitting boots). She was also afforded another opportunity to exchange her boots on 22 June 2006 when the squadron travelled to CFB Esquimalt to receive their claim advances prior to departing to CFB Shilo. The complainant did not choose to exchange kit, nor did she inform anyone that she was still experiencing footwear problems;

The Ops WO's lame excuse may have washed, except for the fact that this young Canadian Forces female member had spend 4 years in Air Cadets with proper fitting boots and she well knew a proper fitting boot from the idiotic boot this Comm Unit was trying to pawn off on her [see Appendix 7].

Also remember that General W.Z. Natynczyk on page 3 of his letter dated 29 January, 2010 confirmed that "I find that the boot fitting procedures set out in the supply manual were not followed by supply personnel at 748 Comm Sqn, Nanaimo" with regard to this young Canadian Forces female member [see Appendix 23].

Appendix 27 [Absolute fabrication by Canadian Forces Y. Couture – young female Canadian Forces member was fired due to plantar fasciitis & she had not started her release]

d.   "On July 11, 2006, the complainant was measured for proper boots, and these were ordered, but the complainant states she never received them." The complainant never received the boots because they were not received by her home unit, 748 Communication Squadron in Esquimalt, BC, until early August 2006: and then the boots were not issued as the complainant had already commenced her release proceedings; and

Yours truly,

Y. Couture
Commander
Director Human Rights and Diversity

Remember that this **young Canadian Forces female member** had grieved her firing by the Canadian Forces due to her plantar fasciitis and not issuing her proper boots so she could perform her military duties, so the letter dated **7 July, 2010 sent to Kathryn Lavery, Early Resolution Advisor, Canadian Human Rights Commission, Suite 1645 Canada Place, 9700 Jasper Avenue, Edmonton, Alberta, Canada T5J 4C3 by Y. Couture, Commander, National Defense Headquarters makes no sense whatsoever.**

This young Canadian Forces female member did not voluntarily seek her release, she **had in fact been fired [released in spite of her protests] by the commanding officer of her Nanaimo, British Columbia, Canada 748 Comm Unit, that being Captain D.R. Bowhey.**

Incredibly, this Kathryn Lavery of the Canadian Human Rights Commission apparently ignores these facts as later chapters will reveal.

Appendix 28 [Canadian Human Rights Commission prejudiced?]

July 17, 2010

Kathryn Lavery, Early Resolution Advisor
Edmonton Regional Office
Canadian Human Rights Commission
#1645 - 9700 Jasper Avenue,
Edmonton, AB T5J 4C3
Kathryn.Lavery@chrc-ccdp.ca

Jennifer Lynch, Chief Commissioner
Gaston Boisvert, Early Resolution Team Leader
Canadian Human Rights Commission
344 Slater Street, 8th Floor,
Ottawa, Ontario K1A 1E1
jennifer.lynch@chrc-ccdp.ca

DND defence letter 7 July, 2010

It doesn't matter what the DND says in its defence.

The independent grievance process dated 29 January, 2010 [you have copy] revealed Specifically, Quote #4 - page 3: General W.Z. Natynczyk in his letter dated 29 January, 2010 confirms that "I find that the boot fitting procedures set out in the supply manual were not followed by supply personnel at 748 Comm Sqn, Nanaimo" which is in direct contradiction to DND defence in its letter dates 7 July item #b in DND defence letter dated July 7, 2010.

If you side with the DND, then you are prejudiced!!

Because "I find that the boot fitting procedures set out in the supply manual were not followed by supply personnel at 748 Comm Sqn, Nanaimo" this caused undue hardship Specifically, Quote #3 - page 3: General W.Z. Natynczyk in his letter dated 29 January, 2010 confirms that because of my congenital condition of Plantar Fasciitis I was qualified for orthopaedic footwear according to Canadian Forces Supply Manual and that, as stated in the Canadian Forces Supply Manual that if improper footwear is given (to a soldier recruit) "improper fitted footwear affects the general well being of an individual, often to such an extent as to impair health, morale and efficiency. It is, therefore, of the utmost importance that

163

individuals wear footwear for which they have been measured and properly fitted".

These problems also included not being able to do the BMQ training because of infected feet - 14 July, 2006 page 000673 of the Canadian Forces Grievance Board file, it clearly indicates in my medical files at Brandon Regional Health Centre/Hospital that I had an infected toe because of the boots I had been issued by my Comm 748 unit "area around blister reddened ... pus" [in my CHRC file].

If you side with the DND, then you are prejudiced!!

And the reason for all this is that I suffered a disability Specifically, Quote #1 - page 3: General W.Z. Natynczyk in his letter dated 29 January, 2010 confirms that my Plantar Fasciitis [pes planus] is congenital "your foot condition is congenital".

Specifically, Quote #2 - page 4: General W.Z. Natynczyk in his letter dated 29 January, 2010 confirms that because of my congenital condition of Plantar Fasciitis I was qualified for orthopaedic footwear according to Canadian Forces Supply Manual "Veteran Affairs Canada defines pes planus, the genetic condition from which you suffer, as a deformed foot. As such, you qualified to be fitted with orthopaedic footwear".

And, instead of giving the remedy for my disability, As you know from my CHRC File #2006-1409 that this occurred on 10 July, 2006 page 000667 of the Canadian Forces Grievance Board file, it clearly indicates in my files at Canadian Forces Base Shilo that Base Surgeon Major Salsman proper fitting boots with "vibram-soles" to accommodate my wide fat feet so I could perform my military duties [copy in my CHRC file] long after I started BMQ training the DND fired me on 3 August, 2007 which is in direct contradiction to the DND defence in its letter dated 7 July item #d where they said I had started release procedures - I never started release procedures -- I WAS FIRED AND NOT GIVEN PROPER BOOTS FOR MY DISABILITY!!

If you side with the DND, then you are prejudiced!!

In fact, in later chapters this young female Canadian Forces member, as far as the author is concerned, had apparently pegged Kathryn Lavery of the Canadian Human Rights Commission most accurately.

It appeared to the author that this Lavery was inclined to accept any "hair-brain" excuse the Canadian Forces fed her and, as far as the author could tell, Lavery ignored all of the evidence presented by this young female Canadian Forces member.

Appendix 29 [Did not resolve any plantar fasciitis discrimination complaint made to Canadian Human Rights Commission]

13 February, 2010

Jennifer Lynch, Chief Commissioner
Gaston Boisvert, Early Resolution Team Leader
Canadian Human Rights Commission
344 Slater Street, 8th Floor,
Ottawa, Ontario K1A 1E1
E-Mail: JENNIFER.LYNCH@CHRC-CCDP.CA
E-Mail: info.com@chrc-ccdp.ca

RE: REACTIVATION OF MY CHRC FILE
       Disability Discrimination CHRC File #2006-1409

Dear Jennifer Lynch,

Finally, my internal grievance with the DND is complete [see final decision letter by General W.Z. Natynczyk dated 29 January, 2010 [Appendix 23 of this book] which denied my grievance [this was to be expected -- the DND never really looked at my underlying discrimination CHRC complaint].

However, as this decision DID NOT resolve any of my discrimination complaints under my CHRC File #2006-1409, I NOW wish to re-activate my Canadian Human Rights Commission file.

There is one good thing about General W.Z. Natynczyk reply in his letter dated 29 January, 2010 -- he does confirm some important matters and proofs establishing my DISCRIMINATION complaints under my CHRC File #2006-1409.

Specifically, Quote #1 - page 3: General W.Z. Natynczyk in his letter dated 29 January, 2010 confirms that my Plantar Fasciitis [pes planus] is congenital "your foot condition is congenital".

Proof of disability: Page 000696 of the Canadian Forces Grievance Board file, Dr. Pistone in his letter dated 22 February, 2007 substantiated that I suffer Bilateral Pes Planus & Posterior tibial dysfunction level 1 [copy in my CHRC file].

Specifically, Quote #2 - page 4: General W.Z. Natynczyk in his letter dated 29 January, 2010 confirms that because of my congenital condition of Plantar Fasciitis I was qualified for orthopaedic footwear according to

Canadian Forces Supply Manual "Veteran Affairs Canada defines pes planus, the genetic condition from which you suffer, as a deformed foot. As such, you qualified to be fitted with orthopaedic footwear".

Specifically, Quote #3 - page 3: General W.Z. Natynczyk in his letter dated 29 January, 2010 confirms that because of my congenital condition of Plantar Fasciitis I was qualified for orthopaedic footwear according to Canadian Forces Supply Manual and that, as stated in the Canadian Forces Supply Manual that if improper footwear is given (to a soldier recruit) "improper fitted footwear affects the general well being of an individual, often to such an extent as to impair health, morale and efficiency. It is, therefore, of the utmost importance that individuals wear footwear for which they have been measured and properly fitted".

Specifically, Quote #4 - page 3: General W.Z. Natynczyk in his letter dated 29 January, 2010 confirms that "I find that the boot fitting procedures set out in the supply manual were not followed by supply personnel at 748 Comm Sqn, Nanaimo".

Specifically, Quote #5 - page 4: General W.Z. Natynczyk in his letter dated 29 January, 2010 confirms that it was Maj. Salsman who diagnosed the need for special boots for me due to my Plantar Fasciitis [pes planus] "I find the earliest opportunity at which you could have been assessed as requiring orthopaedic footwear was upon examination by Maj. Salsman".

As you know from my CHRC File #2006-1409 that this occurred on 10 July, 2006 page 000667 of the Canadian Forces Grievance Board file, it clearly indicates in my files at Canadian Forces Base Shilo that Base Surgeon Major Salsman proper fitting boots with "vibram-soles" to accommodate my wide fat feet so I could perform my military duties [copy in my CHRC file] -- 10 July was long after I started BMQ training.

As you know from my CHRC File #2006-1409 that I suffered grievously due to not being properly fitted with appropriate boots:

-5 July, 2006 there is reference to "Friction marks and hot spots and a blister caused by grossly oversized combat boots" signed by Base Surgeon Major Salsman at CFB Shilo [in my CHRC file].

Page 000688 of the Canadian Forces Grievance Board file, the medical attendant wrote "there is a long friction mark on the posterior ..." followed by "there is also a blister on the plantar ... it appears relatively deep" followed by on the other foot there is a similar friction mark" followed by "hot spots are located on the bottom of the heels" [in my

CHRC file].

- 7 July, 2006 page 000687 of the Canadian Forces Grievance Board file, it clearly indicates I suffered "bilat plantar foot pain" and given medication for this [in my CHRC file]

- 10 July, 2006 page 000667 of the Canadian Forces Grievance Board file, it clearly indicates in my files at Canadian Forces Base Shilo that Base Surgeon Major Salsman proper fitting boots with "vibram-soles" to accommodate my wide fat feet so I could perform my military duties [in my CHRC file].

However, I was never issued these boots to correct my disability of Bilateral Pes Planus & Posterior tibial dysfunction level 1 instead recommended by Base Surgeon Major Salsman.

Specifically, Quote #6 - page 4: General W.Z. Natynczyk in his letter dated 29 January, 2010 confirms that it was Maj. Salsman who diagnosed the need for special boots for me due to my Plantar Fasciitis [pes planus] "and that his recommendation was accepted and acted upon immediately".

This is NOT ACCURATE, in fact I was NEVER issued these boots to correct my disability of Bilateral Pes Planus & Posterior tibial dysfunction level 1 instead, I was released from the Canadian Forces.

As you know from my CHRC File #2006-1409 that I continued to suffer grievously due to not being properly fitted with appropriate boots:

- 14 July, 2006 page 000673 of the Canadian Forces Grievance Board file, it clearly indicates in my medical files at Brandon Regional Health Centre/Hospital that I had an infected toe because of the boots I had been issued by my Comm 748 unit "area around blister reddened ... pus" [in my CHRC file].

In fact, instead of being issued these boots to correct my disability of Bilateral Pes Planus & Posterior tibial dysfunction level 1 and I was released from the Canadian Forces.

The remainder of General W.Z. Natynczyk letter dated 29 January, 2010 is simply a matter of trying to soft-soap the actual facts.

For example, because my 748 Comm Sqn, Nanaimo did not follow the supply manual procedures as confirmed by General W.Z. Natynczyk in his letter dated 29 January, 2010 [as per Quote #4 - page 3] I was instead issued CLOWN SIZED BOOTS that did nothing for my Bilateral Pes Planus & Posterior tibial dysfunction level 1 [colour photo appears as Page 000778 of the Canadian Forces Grievance Board, copy in my CHRC file].

Incredibly, General W.Z. Natynczyk in his letter dated 29 January, 2010 tries to white wash the obvious oversized boots by saying they were a perfect fit as per Quote #7 - Page 3 "the shortest standard sized combat boot that will accommodate your width corresponds exactly to the boot you were issued".

Just look at the CLOWN SIZED BOOTS I was incorrectly issued by my 748 Comm Sqn, Nanaimo unit and tell me if you agree that these are an exact fit!!

General W.Z. Natynczyk comment that these CLOWN SIZED BOOTS are an exact fit is ludicrous!!

In any event, General W.Z. Natynczyk's letter dated 29 January, 2010 and his grievance decision does not address my Disability Discrimination complaint under the CHRC as the Canadian Forces have clearly released me because of my [treatable] disability [Bilateral Pes Planus & Posterior tibial dysfunction level 1] which was easily resolved with proper orthotic insoles [as per Canadian Forces medical directives and Base Surgeon Major Salsman's 10 July, 2006 order - copy in my CHRC file], which I was never issued so I could perform my military duties.

General W.Z. Natynczyk in his letter dated 29 January, 2010 also failed to mention that I spent 4 years in the Air Cadets [2000 - 2004] so I was quite use to "military" requirements and performance.

In addition, General W.Z. Natynczyk in his letter dated 29 January, 2010 failed to mention that I have spent the last several years in the field of security where I routinely wear [combat] boots which have given me no problem with proper orthotics.

Finally, it is very apparent that because of my [treatable] disability [Bilateral Pes Planus & Posterior tibial dysfunction level 1] which was easily resolved with proper orthotic insoles, the discrimination against me continues as the Canadian Forces did not process my application for employment dated 2008 [see below].

In closing, the discrimination against me because of my [treatable] disability [Bilateral Pes Planus & Posterior tibial dysfunction level 1] still continues to this day as the Canadian Forces have not process my application for employment dated 2009 [see below].

Thank you for re-activating my CHRC File #2006-1409 a.s.a.p. as it is not fair that this discrimination continues, as I am being denied a reserve force income since my discriminatory release in 2006 due to my [treatable] disability [Bilateral Pes Planus & Posterior tibial dysfunction level 1], although the Canadian Forces Comm 748 Unit [the employer] was well aware of my [treatable] disability [Bilateral Pes Planus & Posterior tibial dysfunction level 1] which was easily corrected with orthotic insoles BUT NEVER GIVEN SUCH BOOTS although the Canadian Forces medical specialist indicated the need:
- 10 July, 2006 page 000667 of the Canadian Forces Grievance Board file, it clearly indicates in my files at Canadian Forces Base Shilo that Base Surgeon Major Salsman proper fitting boots with "vibram-soles" to accommodate my wide fat feet so I could perform my military duties [in my CHRC file].

And I was denied a reserve force income since my 2008 application was never processed, although the Canadian Forces Comm 748 Unit [the employer] was well aware of my [treatable] disability [Bilateral Pes Planus & Posterior tibial dysfunction level 1] which was Easley corrected with orthotic insoles

And I am being denied any future wage from a regular force position since my 2009 application is not being processed because of my [treatable] disability [Bilateral Pes Planus & Posterior tibial dysfunction level 1] although the Canadian Forces [the employer] is well aware of my [treatable] disability [Bilateral Pes Planus & Posterior tibial dysfunction level 1] which was easily corrected with orthotic insoles:
-General W.Z. Natynczyk in his letter dated 29 January, 2010 failed to mention that I have spent the last several years in the field of security where I routinely wear [combat] boots which have given me no problem with proper orthotics.

The actions of the Canadian Forces in the past [my discriminatory release in 2006, the discriminatory decision not to process my 2008 application] and the continued discrimination by the Canadian Forces in not processing my 2009 application is clearly against my Human Rights in Canada and the United Nations, of which Canada is a signator where I suffer a [treatable] disability [Bilateral Pes Planus & Posterior tibial dysfunction level 1] that has NEVER been addressed by the Canadian Forces in 2006 with my discriminatory release, and their continued insistence not to process my 2008 and 2009 applications when they are well aware of my [treatable] disability [Bilateral Pes Planus & Posterior tibial dysfunction level 1] !!

I wish a correction of this matter through my Disability Discrimination CHRC File #2006-1409 complaint.

Sincerely,

Young female Canadian Forces member

cc. Elmer MacKay
Minister of National Defense

MY APPLICATION IN 2008 FOR THIS JOB WAS NEVER PROCESSED ALTHOUGH I RECEIVED CONFIRMATION FROM THE COMM UNIT IN NANAIMO THAT MY APPLICATION WAS RECEIVED!! DISCRIMINATION STILL CONTINUING BECAUSE OF MY DISABILITY!!!

NEW JOB POSTING
Job Number: 3876022 Title: Radio officer - military (NOC: 1475)
Terms of Employment: Permanent, Part Time leading Full Time, On Call, Weekend, Day, Evening
Salary: $91.28 Daily for 15 hours per week, Other Benefits, Mileage Paid, Medical Benefits, Dental Benefits, Disability Benefits, Life Insurance Benefits, Pension Plan Benefits
Anticipated Start Date: As soon as possible
Location: Nanaimo, British Columbia (2 vacancies)
Skill Requirements:
Education: Completion of high school, Some university, Completion of university
Credentials (certificates, licences, memberships, courses, etc.): Not required
Experience: No experience
Languages: Speak English, Read English, Write English
Work Conditions and Physical Capabilities: Fast-paced environment, Work under pressure, Physically demanding, Attention to detail
Essential Skills: Reading text, Numeracy, Writing, Oral communication, Working with others, Problem solving, Decision making, Critical thinking, Computer use
Other Information: Applicants must hold Canadian Citizenship. For more information, please refer to www.forces.ca
Employer: Canadian Forces Army Reserve Comm 748 Unit
Contact Name: Corporal E.A. Miles
By Mail:

703 Nanaimo Lakes Road
Nanaimo, British Columbia V9R 7B1
By Phone between 9:00 and 16:00:
(250) 755-5360
By E-mail: miles.ea3@forces.gc.ca
How to Apply: Please apply for this job only in the manner specified by
the employer. Failure to do so may result in your application not being
properly considered for the position.
Business Profile: Looking for an exciting change? Your local Army
Reserve is offering both full and part-time opportunities in
Communications & Electronics trades.
Posted 2008/08/07 Advertised until: 2008/08/25

MY APPLICATION IN 2009-2010 SEEMS TO BE IN LIMBO????
DISCRIMINATION STILL CONTINUING BECAUSE OF MY
DISABILITY!!!

RE: how's my application going?
From: ERIC.BILODEAU@forces.gc.ca
Sent: February 1, 2010 5:45:28 AM
Your file is with the processing people. If they did not contact they are
waiting for paper work to get back. They will contact you as soon as they
get everything.

how's my application going?
Sent: February 1, 2010 5:22:59 AM
To: eric.bilodeau@forces.gc.ca
1 February, 2010
Sergeant Eric Bilodeau
Recruitment
Canadian Forces
391 York Avenue, Suite 465
Winnipeg, Manitoba R3C 0P4
eric.bilodeau@forces.gc.ca
Dear Sergeant Bilodeau,
I was wondering what was happening?
I was told in November it would take a couple of days to get my reserve
file from B.C.
However the last word I have from you on 7 January, 2010 is that "your
file is with the processing people. They are waiting for document from

171

previous services. They will contact you when they received them."
I see some of the Direct Entry Officer jobs I have applied for:
First Preference -   DEO Maritime Surface and Sub-surface
Officer
Second Preference -   DEO Aerospace Control Officer
Third Preference -   DEO Intelligence Officer
Fourth Preference -   DEO Military Police Officer
Fifth Preference -   DEO Artillery Officer
Sixth Preference -   DEO Army Officer
Are in high demand:
Jobs Available in Navy
*Maritime Surface and Sub-Surface Officer
*Intelligence Officer
Jobs Available in Air Force
*Aerospace Control Officer
I would even consider non-com spots if need be:
2010 TV Ads
Wanted : Air Traffic Controllers
Wanted : Aircraft Technicians
Wanted : Artillery Soldiers
Wanted : Electronic Technicians
Wanted : Mechanics
Wanted : Sonar Operators
Do you know when my application will be processed?
Thank you,
Young female Canadian Forces member

Appendix 30 [Kathryn Lavery of Canadian Human Rights processing plantar fasciitis complaints]

CANADIAN COMMISSION
HUMAN RIGHTS CANADIENNE DES
COMMISSION DROITS DE LA PERSONNE

Resolution Services Division   Division des services de règlement

March 31, 2010

File number: 20061409

Dear Ms.

I am writing in response to your email of March 26, 2010, addressed to the Chief Commissioner. Please be advised that your registered letter dated February 13, 2010, to the Chief Commissioner has been located, and it was forwarded to the officer assigned to your file, Ms. Kathryn Lavery, who has added it to your file.

Ms. Lavery is continuing to process your file. If you have any questions about the Commission's procedures regarding reactivating a complaint when an alternate redress procedure has been exhausted, Ms. Lavery would be pleased to answer your questions.

You may contact Ms. Lavery at (780) 495-6350.

Yours sincerely,

Gaston Boisvert
Early Resolution Team Leader

244 Slater Street, Ottawa, Ontario K1A 1E1
344, rue Slater, Ottawa (Ontario) K1A 1E1
www.chrc-ccdp.ca

Appendix 31 [Gaston Boisvert of Canadian Human Rights Commission says he will not be looking at the substance of plantar fasciitis complaint]

CANADIAN COMMISSION
HUMAN RIGHTS CANADIENNE DES
COMMISSION DROITS DE LA PERSONNE

Resolution Services Division   Division des services de règlement

MAR 1 9 2010

File number: 20061409

Dear Ms.

This is further to our letter of April 21, 2009 regarding your complaint against the Canadian Forces.

This complaint came before the Commission in April 2009. The Commission decided not to deal with the complaint at that time under section 41(1)(a) of the *Canadian Human Rights Act*. You were advised that, at the end of the other procedure, you could ask the Commission to reactivate the complaint.

Because you have asked that the complaint be reactivated, the matter will be re-submitted to the Commission at an upcoming meeting.

Before re-submitting the complaint to the Commission, I am inviting you to provide your position on the issues for decision. To assist you, I have attached information on the factors the Commission will consider when making its decision. Please note that the Commission will not be addressing the substance of the complaint at this time, i.e., it will not be considering evidence related to the allegations of discrimination. Its review will be limited exclusively to the issues raised under section 41(1)(d).

Please review the attached information carefully before preparing your reply. Your reply should address only what is relevant to the decision at this time, not the substance of the allegations. Please limit your reply to ten (10) pages, not including attachments, and please send it to Ms. Kathryn Lavery at the **address below by May 7, 2010**. In order to avoid delay in the handling of this matter, extensions to this period will not be granted except in extraordinary circumstances.

...2

Suite 1645 Canada Place, 9700 Jasper Avenue, Edmonton, Alberta T5J 4C3
Pièce 1645, Place du Canada, 9700, avenue Jasper, Edmonton (Alberta) T5J 4C3
Tel./tél. (780) 495-4040 br/ou 1-800-999-6899, TTY/ATS 1-888-643-3304, Fax/téléc. (780) 495-4044
www.chrc-ccdp.ca

Once we have received the parties' positions on the issues for decision, a report to the Commission will be prepared. This report will be disclosed to the parties before it is submitted to the Commission, and they will be given an opportunity to make written submissions. Any submissions we receive will be put to the Commission along with the report.

I wish to confirm receipt of your letters dated 23 February, 2010, and 26 February, 2010, addressed to the Commission, as well as your many emails. You have already provided much information to the Commission on the matters at hand. I am sending you this letter and attached factors sheet in case you wish to submit additional information on the issues that the Commission will be considering. Please be assured that the information you have already provided will be considered during the drafting of the Section 40/41 Report.

Please note that the parties should preserve any material related to the allegations of discrimination, including information in electronic formats, until the final disposition of the matter.

If you have any questions, please contact Kathryn Lavery, Early Resolution Advisor, at (780) 495-6350.

Yours sincerely,

Gaston Boisvert
Early Resolution Team Leader

Encl.   Complaint form (with revised Summary of Complaint)
Information on section 41 issues for decision

Suite 1645 Canada Place, 9700 Jasper Avenue, Edmonton, Alberta T5J 4C3
Pièce 1645, Place du Canada, 9700, avenue Jasper, Edmonton (Alberta) T5J 4C3
Tél./tél. (780) 495-4040 or/ou 1-800-999-6899, TTY/ATS 1-888-643-3304, Fax/téléc. (780) 495-4044
www.chrc-ccdp.ca

Appendix 32 [Canadian Forces says fasciitis complaint frivolous]

"The CF submits that the complaint is both trivial and frivolous. The acts complained of do not constitute discriminatory practices under the *CHRA*, nor do they raise any issues of public interest that would be served by the Commission dealing with the complaint. Adjudication of this complaint will not advance in any way the purpose of the *CHRA*. There is no evidence that the CF discriminated against the complainant or that her footwear problem was in any way relevant to her unsatisfactory performance.

Appendix 33 [Canadian Forces grievance said plantar fasciitis complaint not in public interest]

36. In its independent review of the complainant's grievance, the CFGB examined: "whether the grievor's release under item 5(d) of the table to the *Queen's Regulations and Orders for the Canadian Forces* (QR&O) article 15.01 was justified and appropriate in the circumstances." In the course of its review, the CFGB also examined whether the CF had discriminated against the complainant within the meaning of the *CHRA*, and it reached the following conclusion at page 18 of its report dated September 30, 2008:

> "Simply stated, there is no evidence before the Board to support a finding that the CF discriminated against the grievor either upon the grounds of her alleged disability or, as suggested at one stage, because she was a woman. The Board recommends that this aspect of the grievance be rejected."

45. The Canadian Forces Grievance Board, an administrative tribunal external and independent from the Canadian Forces, conducted a review of the complainant's grievance and examined whether the complainant was accommodated for her foot disability and whether her RTU and release from the Reserve Force were related to her foot disability. It concluded that she was appropriately accommodated for her foot disability in that she was not required to wear combat boots by the third day of her course, that she was measured for properly fitting boots and that these were ordered, but that she was returned to unit before she received the boots and subsequently released. It also concluded that her release was based on her unsatisfactory performance at the BMQ course, and that her unsatisfactory performance was not related to ill-fitting boots. These are the same issues as those raised in the present complaint. The Canadian Forces Grievance Board also concluded that there was no evidence that the complainant had been discriminated against on the grounds of disability and/or gender within the meaning of the *CHRA*. The Chief of the Defence Staff, who is the Final Authority, accepted the Board's conclusions and recommendations, and denied the grievance and the complainant's request for financial compensation.

46. It appears that the Canadian Forces Grievance Board, an independent administrative tribunal, and the Final Authority did, in fact, turn their minds to all of the human rights issues raised in the present complaint and addressed them, and it would therefore not be in the public interest for the Commission to deal with this complaint.

Appendix 34 [Davis Langtry of Canadian Human Rights Commission, without looking at the substance of the plantar fasciitis complaint, rules the complaint is frivolous]

CANADIAN   COMMISSION
HUMAN RIGHTS   CANADIENNE DES
COMMISSION   DROITS DE LA PERSONNE

Record of Decision Under Sections 40/41

Complaint Information

File Number: 20061409

Date of Complaint: November 27, 2006

Complainant:

Respondent: Canadian Forces

Decision under section 41(1)

The Commission decided for the reason(s) identified below, not to deal with the complaint under section 41(1)(d) of the *Canadian Human Rights Act*, because the complaint is trivial, frivolous, vexatious or made in bad faith.

Signature

Deputy Chief Commissioner   August 25, 2010

                                               Date

Appendix 35 [Can complain to Federal Court, but Canadian Human Rights Commission does not have to defend its ruling]

CANADIAN HUMAN RIGHTS
COMMISSION

COMMISSION CANADIENNE
DES DROITS DE LA PERSONNE

Deputy Chief Commissioner

Vice-président

PROTECTED B

SEP 1 0 2010

Dear Ms.

I am writing to inform you of the decision taken by the Canadian Human Rights Commission in your complaint (20061409) against Canadian Forces.

Before rendering the decision, the Commission reviewed the report disclosed to you previously and any submission(s) filed in response to the report. After examining this information, the Commission decided, pursuant to paragraph 41(1)(d) of the *Canadian Human Rights Act*, not to deal with the complaint.

The decisions of the Commission are attached.

Accordingly, the file on this matter has now been closed.

If you have any questions please do not hesitate to contact Ha Lam, Commission Meeting Unit, at (613) 943-9530 or by email: ha.lam@chrc-ccdp.ca.

For your information, either party to a complaint can ask the Federal Court to review a Commission's decision under subsection 18(1) of the *Federal Courts Act*. The application to the Court must normally be filed within 30 days of receipt of the Commission's decision. Also, please note that the Court has found that the Commission cannot be a respondent in a judicial review of its own decision. Please refer to Rule 303(1) of the Federal Courts Rules, which indicates that an applicant shall name as a respondent every person directly affected by the order sought in the application, other than the tribunal whose decision is under review. To enquire about the procedures, please contact the Federal Court office in Ottawa at (613) 992-4238 or visit the website at www.fct-cf.gc.ca.

Yours sincerely,

David Langtry

Encl.

344 Slater Street
344, rue Slater
Ottawa, Canada K1A 1E1

Canada

180

Appendix 36 [Running shoes make it alright?]

As noted, both Lavery and Langtry apparently felt that the rationales used by the Canadian Forces to indicate this young female Canadian Forces member was well treated by the Canadian Forces was their ["rather stupid"] comment that she was allowed to use running shoes to complete her BMQ [see Appendix 33 for Lavery's comment and see Appendix 36 for Langtry's comment] that is sufficient.

This is Lavery's comment:

45. The Canadian Forces Grievance Board, an administrative tribunal external and independent from the Canadian Forces, conducted a review of the complainant's grievance and examined whether the complainant was accommodated for her foot disability and whether her RTU and release from the Reserve Force were related to her foot disability. It concluded that she was appropriately accommodated for her foot disability in that she was not required to wear combat boots by the third day of her course, that she was measured for properly fitting boots

This is Langtry's comment:

The Canadian Forces Grievance Board, an administrative tribunal external and independent from the Canadian Forces, conducted a review of the complainant's grievance and examined whether the complainant was accommodated for her foot disability and whether her RTU and release from the Reserve Force were related to her foot disability. It concluded that she was appropriately accommodated for her foot disability in that she was not required to wear combat boots by the third day of her course, that she was measured for properly fitting boots and that

Signature

Deputy Chief Commissioner

August 25, 2010

Date

181

**Appendix 37 [Cost of orthotics was the deciding factor in the
Canadian Human Rights Commission not looking at the substance of
the plantar fasciitis complaint]**

grievor claims that she complained about her boots to personnel at the unit, but they took no
ective action (p.486). She also requested additional remedies:

5. Reimbursement of $330.00 for foot-casts related to my disability flat feet / *plantar
fasciitis* to prepare inserts for all my footwear ...

6. Payment of whatever other Orthotic inserts that may be required ...

TERRY W. MALLENBY RESUME

Former State Facility Operations Manager – Secure Custody Young Offenders
Former Classification Officer – Maximum Security Adult Penitentiary
Former Federal Manpower Immigration Counselor
Act/Dist. Manager Child Protection Social Services
Cited in National Library of Medicine
Listed in City University of Hong Kong Library
Referenced in Bodleian Law Library
Listed in Loyola University Chicago Library
Referenced in Cambridge University Library
Cited in Metropolitan Toronto Reference Library
Published Doctoral Dissertation - UMI
"Expert Witness" Supreme Court of B.C. [1973]

**The BC Penitentiary, an imposing granite fortress along
the main thoroughfare between Coquitlam and New Westminster.**

The Officer Down Memorial - dedicated to each and every law enforcement officer
who have had their life taken while in the performance of their duties.
Classification Officer Mary Steinhauser
Department of Corrections
Cause of Death: Gunfire
End of Watch: June 11, 1975
Age: 32
Mary Steinhauser was shot to death as guards rushed prisoners holding her hostage.
She was employed at the British Columbia Penitentiary at the time of her death.

183

National Center for Biotechnology Information, U.S. National Library of Medicine

Facilitating the disappearance of perceptual error to the Poggendorff illusion.
Mallenby TW. Lang Speech. 1976 Apr-Jun;19(2):193-9.
PMID: 1018566 [PubMed - indexed for MEDLINE]

The personal space of hard-of-hearing children after extended contact with 'normals'.
Mallenby TW, Mallenby RG.
Br J Soc Clin Psychol. 1975 Sep;14(3):253-7.
PMID: 1182405 [PubMed - indexed for MEDLINE]

The effect of extended contact with "normals" on the social behavior of hard-of-hearing children.
Mallenby TW.
J Soc Psychol. 1975 Feb;95(First Half):137-8.
PMID: 1113519 [PubMed - indexed for MEDLINE]

Effect of discussion on reduction of magnitude of Poggendorff illusion.
Mallenby TW.
Percept Mot Skills. 1974 Oct;39(2):787-91.
PMID: 4453496 [PubMed - indexed for MEDLINE]

Personal space: projective and direct measures with institutionalized mentally retarded children.
Mallenby TW.
J Pers Assess. 1974 Feb;38(1):28-31.
PMID: 4592504 [PubMed - indexed for MEDLINE]

A note on perceived self-acceptance of institutionalized mentally retarded (IMR) children.
Mallenby TW.
J Genet Psychol. 1973 Sep;123(1st Half):171-2.
PMID: 4593476 [PubMed - indexed for MEDLINE]

City University of Hong Kong Library

A bibliography of research on spatial and social behaviour / compiled by
Terry W. Mallenby, Ruth G. Roberts.
Thomas Todd Press, c1973.
Shatin Storage, Call # C0237118

Oxford University, Bodleian Libraries:

Canada's criminal justice system : guilty until proved innocent : case study from Cour Supérieure
en matière de faillite, Palais de Justice (Montreal), File #500-11-002290-894
Terry Wallice Mallenby
Publication Date: 1990
Aleph System Number: 010456749

Nicole Bomberg, an investigator with the Ant-Discrimination [sic] Directorate of the Public
Service Commission of Canada purposefully lies in a letter dated 26 August, 1983 to hide the fact
that false murder charge statements were made ..
Terry Wallice Mallenby

Publication Date: 1990
Aleph System Number: 010458715

Alberta crown agent RAE Kubik's legacy to Canada : more fabricated statements by government agent(s)
Terry Wallice Mallenby.
Publication Date: 1999
Aleph System Number: 013699710

Incidents of physical assault against child-abuse investigation workers : the nature of child-abuse protection legislation as a possible reason for such incidents
 Further information: some Canadian provincial examples of internal policies attempting to deal with such incidents: placing the trend of such incidents in a theoretical perspective, by Terry W. Mallenby
Author:Mallenby, Terry W., 1947-
Publisher Details: Thesis (doctoral)--Kensington University, 1994
Subjects:Child abuse -- Law and legislation -- United States ; Child abuse -- Law and legislation -- Canada; Child abuse -- United States -- Investigation ; Child abuse -- Canada -- Investigation ; Social workers -- Crimes against
 Aleph System Number: 011403458

Loyola University Chicago Library

"$275,000 of taxpayer's money wasn't enough!" : the federal government of Canada conspiracy
Terry Wallice Mallenby.
Wallice Institute of Psychometric Assessment, 1999.
Subjects:Political persecution--Canada--Case studies.
Judicial error--Canada--Case studies.
False testimony--Canada--Case studies.
Misconduct in office--Canada--Case studies.
Location: Cudahy Main Stacks
Call Number: KE9440 .M23 T86 1999

Cambridge University Library

Complete discharge from bankruptcy, including preferred Canadian and Quebec student loans, due to false statements by the Royal Canadian Mounted Police
Terry Wallice Mallenby
Institute of Psychometric Assessment, 1990.
Subject(s):
Bankruptcy -- Canada.
Royal Canadian Mounted Police.
Tort liability of police -- Canada.
Call # 1992.11.299

Dealing with a violent work environment : internal policies and legislation dealing with physical assault and other threats against child protective social workers / Terry W. Mallenby.
Distributed by Institute of Psychometric Assessment, Applied Studies & Investigative Research, 1994.
ISBN: 0969594402

Subject(s):
Abused children -- Services for -- United States.
Abused children -- Services for -- Canada.
Social workers -- Crimes against -- United States.
Social workers -- Crimes against -- Canada.
Call # 1995.10.275

Child abuse: a beginning social worker's understanding and use of the DSM-III-R and three
reactive mental disorders following child abuse : reactive attachment disorder, post-traumatic
stress disorder, and adjustment disorder
Terry W. Mallenby
Distributed by Instiutute of Psychometric Assessment, 1994.
Subject(s):
Adjustment disorders in children.
Attachment behaviour in children.
Child abuse.
Post-traumatic stress disorder in children.
Call # 1998.10.411

Metropolitan Toronto Reference Library

How to make staff safe: how to reduce labour-management conflict: how to reduce staff
grievances
By Terry W. Mallenby
Year: 1997, Book, 2 v.
 Subjects:
•Child abuse--Investigation.
•Child welfare workers--Training of.
•Child welfare--Administration.
•Social work administration.
•Social work with children--Administration.
•Social workers--Training of.
•Violence in the workplace.
•Violence--Forecasting.
2 copies
Reference only - not holdable
ISBN: 0969594402
Call # 361.3068 M12 1997 V. 1
Call #361.3068 M12 1997 V. 2

WorldCat is the world's largest library catalog

Cognitive development: the functional aspect of symbolization and language,
by Terry W Mallenby
Winnipeg, S. Evans, ©1973.
Database: WorldCat

Personal space : direct measurement techniques with hard-of-hearing children
by Terry W Mallenby
Publisher: Sage Publications, 1974.
Database: WorldCat

The effect of verbal mediation on the reduction of error to the Poggendorff illusion
by Terry W Mallenby
Publication: Bulletin of the Psychonomic Society, v5 n2 (19750205): 170-172
Database: CrossRef

Teach your child to read : a simple method for parents and educators
by Terry W Mallenby
Institute of Applied Studies, 1984.
Database: WorldCat

The relative effectiveness of whole- and part-task simulators
by Terry Mallenby
Institute of Applied Studies, 1984.
Database: WorldCat

Using the minnesota multiphasic personality inventory (MMPI) to determine the suitability of an inmate for parole, release or temporary absence.
by Terry Mallenby
Institute of Applied Studies 1984.
Database: WorldCat

When the "baby-boom" cohort reaches 65 : will it be social chaos or a carefully planned transition : an introductory research proposal
by Terry W Mallenby
Institute of Psychometric Assessment & Applied Studies, 1986.
Database: WorldCat

Quality assurance in medical/health care utilizing and incorporating three methods of evaluation: process, setting and outcome : an introduction to assessing medical/health care by means of a conceptual "process matrix" : with special reference to acute care and chronic care hospitals
by Terry W Mallenby
Institute of Psychometric Assessment and Applied Studies, 1986.
Database: WorldCat

Human rights violations in Canada : individual being denied employment with the Federal Government of Canada due to false "murder charge" statements made by M.J. Hauser of the Correctional Service of Canada and by Nicole Bomberg of the Public Service Commission of Canada : (continuing case study from Cour supérieure en matière de faillite, Palais de justice, Montréal, File #500-11-002290-894) : can the new Solicitor General of Canada, Hon. Pierre Cadiuex, correct the damage and have this individual re-hired by the Federal Government of Canada?
by Terry Wallice Mallenby
Institute of Psychometric Assessment, Applied Studies and Investigative Research, 1990
Database: WorldCat

Complete discharge from bankruptcy, including preferred Canadian and Quebec student loans, due to false statements by the Royal Canadian Mounted Police...
by Terry Mallenby
Institute of Psychometric Assessment, 1990.
Database: WorldCat

Dealing with a violent work environment : internal policies and legislation dealing with physical assault and other threats against child protective social workers
by Terry W Mallenby
Institute of Psychometric Assessment, Applied Studies & Investigative Research, 1994
Database: WorldCat

Child abuse : a beginning social worker's understanding and use of the DSM-III-R and three reactive mental disorders following child abuse : reactive attachment disorder, post-traumatic stress disorder, and adjustment disorder
by Terry Wallice Mallenby
Institute of Psychometric Assessment, 1994.
Database: WorldCat

Incidents of physical assault against child-abuse investigation workers: the nature of child-abuse protection legislation as a possible reason for such incidents
by Terry W Mallenby
Thesis/dissertation : Thesis/dissertation
Publisher: Ann Arbor : UMI, 1994.
Database: WorldCat

R.C.M.P. Sgt. John ("Jack") Thomas Randle's legacy to Canada.
by Terry W Mallenby
Institute of Psychometric Assessment, Applied Studies & Investigative Research, 1996
Database: WorldCat

Complete discharge from bankruptcy including preferred student loans due to Royal Canadian Mounted Police harassment : a most unusual case of bankruptcy.
by Terry W Mallenby
Wallice Institute of Psychometric Assessment, 1997
Database: WorldCat

How to make staff safe: how to reduce labour-management conflict : how to reduce staff grievances
by Terry W Mallenby
Wallice Institute of Psychometric Assessment & Applied Studies, 1997?
Database: WorldCat

Human rights violations in Canada by federal agents of the Canadian Human Rights Anti-Discrimination Agency of the Public Service Commission of Canada.
by Terry W Mallenby
Wallice Institute of Psychometric Assessment, 1997.
Database: WorldCat

The Newfoundland Department of Social Services is the worst department this author has ever read about.
by Terry W Mallenby
Wallice Institute of Psychometric Assessment, 1997.
Database: WorldCat

"Is he Canada's example of another Mark Furman : R.C.M.P. Sgt. John ("Jack") Thomas Randle purposefully committed lies, fabricated evidence, made false statements & committed illegal acts!"
by Terry W Mallenby
Wallice Institute of Psychometric Assessment & Applied Studies, 1997
Database: WorldCat

One of the worst social service departments this author has ever seen; receiving a lot of bad press for ignoring cruelly abused children and staff concerns about safety
by Terry W Mallenby
Wallice Institute of Psychometric Assessment, 1997
Database: WorldCat

Is it an example of unethical behavior by two psychiatrists? What do you think?.
by Terry W Mallenby
Wallice Institute of Psychometric Assessment, 1997.
Database: WorldCat

Judge John Gomery's inappropriate comments based on lies, false statements, fabricated statements & illegal acts by R.C.M.P. Sgt. John Thomas Randle.
by Terry W Mallenby
Wallice Institute of Psychometric Assessment & Applied Studies, 1998.
Database: WorldCat

Can police harassment involving illegal acts, false statements and fabricated evidence lead to a diagnosis of post-traumatic stress disorder sufficient to approve permanent disability pension?.
by Terry W Mallenby
Wallice Institute of Psychometric Assessment & Applied Studies, 1998.
Database: WorldCat

Is it an example of unethical behavior by a psychologist? What do you think?
by Terry W Mallenby
Wallice Institute of Psychometric Assessment & Applied Studies, 1998.
Database: WorldCat

Royal Canadian Mounted Police officers Sgt. John ("Jack") Thomas Randle's & Cpl. Jackett's legacy to Canada.
by Terry W Mallenby
Wallice Institute of Psychometric Assessment, 1998.
Database: WorldCat

Canadian anti-discriminate [sic] directorate and Canadian public service staff Nicole Bomberg's legacy to Canada.
by Terry W Mallenby
Wallice Institute of Psychometric Assessment, 1998.
Database: WorldCat

Federal government of Canada staff lies cost Canadian taxpayers plenty!
by Terry W Mallenby
Wallice Institute of Psychometric Assessment, 1998.
Database: WorldCat

Canadian anti-discrimination directorate and Canadian public service staff Lorisa Stein's legacy to Canada.
by Terry W Mallenby
Wallice Institute of Psychometric Assessment, 1998.
Database: WorldCat

Kofi Annan, Secretary General of the United Nations and Mary Robinson, the Human Rights Commissioner : their legacy to the world
by Terry W Mallenby
Wallice Institute of Psychometric Assessment, 1998.
Database: WorldCat

"$275,000 of taxpayer's money wasn't enough!": the federal government of Canada conspiracy
by Terry W Mallenby
Wallice Institute of Psychometric Assessment, 1999
Database: WorldCat

"Alberta premier Ralph Klein's legacy to Canadian criminal justice!"
by Terry Wallice Mallenby
Wallice Institute of Psychometric Assessment, 1999
Database: WorldCat

Alberta crown agent RAE Kubik's legacy to Canada : more fabricated statements by government agent(s)
by Terry W Mallenby
Wallice Institute of Psychometric Assessment, 1999.
Database: WorldCat

The story 'too hot' for the investigative program "The Fifth Estate"!!
by Terry W Mallenby
Wallice Institute of Psychometric Assessment, Applied Studies & Investigative Research, 2000.
Database: WorldCat

Cognitive development : the efficacy of the A Plus Child Development's Project "Head Start"
Program in such development : a review of the "Head Start" Program
by Terry W Mallenby
Institute of Applied Studies, 2002.
Database: WorldCat

Military issue: "bandaged heels & grossly over-sized combat boots"
by Terry Mallenby
Wallice Institute of Psychometric Assessment, 2010.
Database: WorldCat

General W.Z. Natynczyk says "boot fitting procedures were not followed by 748 Comm Sqn,
Nanaimo"
by Terry W Mallenby
Institute of Psychometric Assessment, 2010.
Database: WorldCat

Canada's police force: lies, fabrication, perjury ... and much worse?
by Terry Mallenby
Publisher: Charleston, South Carolina : CreateSpace, 2012
Database: WorldCat

EDUCATIONAL BACKGROUND OF TERRY W. MALLENBY:

OFFICE DE LA LANGUE FRANCAISE:
GOUVERNEMENT DU QUEBEC, OFFICE DE LA LANGUE FRANCAISE ATTESTATION
CERTIFICATE #41-0063, DATED 24 MARS, 1986. CONFORMEMENT A L'ARTICLE 35 DE
LA CHARTE DE LA LANGUE FRANCAISE, NOUS ATTESTONS QUE TERRY
MALLENBY POSSEDE DE LA LANGUE OFFICIELLE DU QUEBEC UNE
CONNAISSANCE APPROPRIEE A L'EXERCISE DE SA PROFESSION.

MINISTERE DE L'EDUCATION:
GOUVERNEMENT DU QUEBEC, MINISTERE DE L'EDUCATION RELEVE DES ACQUIS,
DATED JUILLET, 1990
FRENCH SECOND LANGUAGE: LEVEL 1, 2 & 3.

DIPLOMA GENERAL SOCIAL WORK, DIPLOMA DATED 8 OCTOBER, 1974
DIPLOMA APPLIED PSYCHOLOGY, DIPLOMA DATED 13 MAY, 1975
CANADIAN INSTITUTE OF SCIENCE & TECHNOLOGY [NOW CALLED "GRANTON
INSTITUTE OF TECHNOLOGY"]. COURSES: PEOPLE IN GROUPS; CONFLICT &
CHANGE; SOCIOLOGY AS A SCIENCE & SOCIAL WORK HISTORY; SOCIAL
INSTITUTIONS, SOCIAL CONTROL & PROBLEMS OF COMMUNICATION; CONCEPTS,
METHODS & MODELS; SOCIAL PROCESSES & SOCIAL PROBLEMS; ADAPTATION &
HUMAN RELATIONS; PRACTICAL & APPLIED PSYCHOLOGY; GENERAL
INDUSTRIAL PSYCHOLOGY; TRAINING FOR MANAGEMENT & MENTAL
EFFICIENCY; VOCATIONAL TESTING & INTERVIEWING; INTER-GROUP RELATIONS;
THE REVERSE EFFECT.

CERTIFICATE JAIL ADMINISTRATION, CERTIFICATE DATED: 09 FEB, 1976
CERTIFICATE JAIL OPERATIONS, CERTIFICATE DATED: 01 MARCH, 1976
U.S. DEPARTMENT OF JUSTICE, NATIONAL INSTITUTE OF CORRECTIONS, BUREAU
OF PRISONS. COURSES: ADMINISTRATION OF OPERATIONS; PERSONNEL & FISCAL
MANAGEMENT; COMMUNITY RELATIONS & JAIL PLANNING; CORRECTIONAL
HISTORY & JAIL CLIMATE; SUPERVISION, DISCIPLINE & SPECIAL PRISONERS.

CERTIFICATE DRUGS & YOUTH COUNSELING, CERTIFICATE MARCH, 1975
CERTIFICATE ADVANCED CORRECTIONAL COUNSELING, CERT. SEPT., 1975
DOUGLAS COLLEGE. [REFERENCE LETTER BY: R.E. WATKINS, CLASSIFICATION
SERVICES COORDINATOR, DATED 1 OCTOBER, 1975]. COURSES: ADVANCED
INTERVIEWING & COUNSELING; MARRIAGE & FAMILY COUNSELING; PROBLEMS
OF VIOLENCE; PAROLE PREDICTION & SUPERVISION; MEASUREMENT &
EVALUATION OF RESEARCH TECHNIQUES; BUREAUCRACIES & CONFLICT;
COMMUNITY LIAISON SERVICES; COMPULSORY INTERVIEWING, INMATE CODE &
RESTRICTIONS; PAROLE VIOLATION & FORFEITURE; RADICAL THERAPIES &
POLYGRAPH.

BACHELOR OF ARTS PSYCHOLOGY
SIMON FRASER UNIVERSITY, DEGREE DATED: MAY, 1970. [REGIONALLY
ACCREDITED UNIVERSITY] [COMPLETED IN CANADA][EVALUATED TO U.S.A.
EQUIVALENCY BY EDUCATIONAL RECORDS EVALUATION SERVICE,

SACRAMENTO, CALIFORNIA][LETTER DATED 10 JANUARY, 1996, REFERENCE #95-01008]
[SIMON FRASER UNIVERSITY RANKING #1, FOR CANADIAN MEDIUM SIZED UNIVERSITIES, MACLEAN'S RANKINGS][LETTER OF REFERENCE BY: DR. H. WEINBERG, ASSOCIATE PROFESSOR, DATED 24 FEBRUARY, 1970][LETTER OF REFERENCE BY: DR. ELINOR AMES, ASSOCIATE PROFESSOR, DATED 17 MARCH, 1971]. COURSES (MATHEMATICS, ENGLISH, OTHER): MATH 101 STATISTICS; MATH 114 FUNDAMENTAL MATH II; ENGL 201 THE STUDY OF LITERATURE; PHIL 100 THEORY OF KNOWLEDGE; EDUC 201 THEORY OF EDUCATION; CC&A 200 THEORY AND PROCESS OF COMMUNICATION; PSA 274 TRADITIONAL ECONOMICS & TECHNOLOGY; PSA 172 ANTHROPOLOGICAL CONCEPTS; BSF 425 LEARNING AND THE PROCESS OF EDUCATION. COURSES (GENERAL & ADVANCED PSYCHOLOGY): PSYC 150 FACTORS OF PERFORMANCE; PSYC 201 EXPERIMENTAL PSYCHOLOGY; PSYC 210 DATA ANALYSIS IN PSYCHOLOGY; PSYC 220 LEARNING; PSYC 230 PERCEPTION; PSYC 240 MOTIVATION; PSYC 320 COGNITIVE PROCESSES; PSYC 325 MEMORY; PSYC 330 SITUATION PERCEPTION; PSYC 340 PSYCHOPATHOLOGY; PSYC 350 DEVELOPMENTAL PSYCHOLOGY; PSYC 360 SOCIAL PSYCHOLOGY; PSYC 370 THEORIES OF PERSONALITY; PSYC 380 PHYSIOLOGICAL PSYCHOLOGY; PSYC 401 HISTORY & SYSTEMS; PSYC 450 DEVELOPMENTAL PSYCHOLOGY SEMINAR; PSYC 480 PHYSIOLOGICAL PSYCHOLOGY SEMINAR. PSYC 310 THEORY OF MEASUREMENT [TESTING EXPERIENCE: WECHSLER INTELLIGENCE SCALE FOR CHILDREN (W.I.S.C.); WECHSLER ADULT INTELLIGENCE SCALE (W.A.I.S.)]; PSYC 496 DIRECTED STUDIES ["EPIDEMIOLOGY OF MENTAL ILLNESS"; NOTE: THE PROJECT FOR DIRECTED STUDIES CONSISTED OF A PATIENT FILE REVIEW OF A PSYCHIATRIC HOSPITAL RELATED TO DETERMINING THE EPIDEMIOLOGY OF MENTAL ILLNESS COMPLETED IN CONJUNCTION WITH FELLOW STUDENT MS. MARY STEINHAUSER WHO WAS LATER SHOT TO DEATH DURING A HOSTAGE INCIDENT AT THE B.C. PENITENTIARY WHERE WE BOTH WORKED].

BACHELOR OF SOCIAL WORK
MCGILL UNIVERSITY, DEGREE DATED: 8 NOVEMBER, 1988. [REGIONALLY ACCREDITED UNIVERSITY][COMPLETED IN CANADA][EVALUATED TO U.S.A. EQUIVALENCY BY EDUCATIONAL RECORDS EVALUATION SERVICE, SACRAMENTO, CALIFORNIA][LETTER DATED 10 JANUARY, 1996, REFERENCE #95-01008][MCGILL UNIVERSITY RANKING #1, LARGE SIZED UNIVERSITIES IN CANADA, MACLEAN'S RANKINGS][REFERENCE LETTER BY: DR. IRV BINIK, ASSOCIATE PROFESSOR, DATED 6 JUNE, 1986]
[REFERENCE LETTER BY: MRS. LYNN THOMPSON, DATED 27 NOV., 1987][REFERENCE LETTER BY: PETER LEONARD, DIRECTOR, DATED 30 MAY, 1988]. COURSES IN SOCIAL WORK: SW 350 SOCIAL WORK SKILLS LABORATORY; SW 352 PUBLIC SOCIAL SERVICES IN CANADA; SW 353 SOCIAL WORK PRACTICE; SW 354 SOCIAL SERVICES IN HEALTH FIELD; SW 355 FIELD PRACTICE I [SENIOR CITIZENS]; SW 356 FIELD PRACTICE II [SENIOR CITIZENS]; SW 364 INDUSTRIAL SOCIAL WORK; SW 458 SOCIAL POLICY & ADMINISTRATION; SW 420 ADVANCED FIELD PRACTICE I [CHILD PROTECTION]; SW 421 ADVANCED FIELD PRACTICE II [CHILD PROTECTION]; SW 459 ADULT-CHILD SEXUAL RELATIONS: LEGAL ISSUES; SW 475 COMMUNITY ORGANIZATIONS; SW 492 SEMINAR ON FAMILY VIOLENCE; SW 484 SEMINAR ON COMMUNITY ORGANIZATIONS; SW 530 SEMINAR ON SOCIAL PERSPECTIVES OF AGING;

[VOLUNTARY PLACEMENT PRIOR TO PROGRAM AT DOUGLAS PSYCHIATRIC HOSPITAL A MCGILL UNIVERSITY TEACHING HOSPITAL, CONFIRMATION LETTER BY D. DELANEY, DATED 21 NOVEMBER, 1986].

POST-GRADUATE DIPLOMA HEALTH & SOCIAL SERVICES MANAGEMENT, MCGILL UNIVERSITY [DIPLOMA DATED: 7 JUNE, 1988; REGIONALLY ACCREDITED UNIVERSITY][MCGILL UNIVERSITY RANKING #1, LARGE SIZED UNIVERSITIES IN CANADA, MACLEAN'S RANKINGS][LETTER OF REFERENCE BY: DR. H. COOPERSMITH M.D., ASSISTANT PROFESSOR, DATED 11 NOV., 1987][LETTER OF REFERENCE BY: MR. ROBERT VYNCKE, VILLE MARIE SOCIAL SERVICES, YOUTH PROTECTION, 11 DEC., 1987][LETTER OF REFERENCE BY: MR. ROBIN ELEY, MBA, CA, DIRECTOR, DATED 24 MAY, 1988]
COURSES: 627-101 COLLEGE ALGEBRA & FUNCTIONS; 279-294 LABOR MANAGEMENT RELATIONS; 619-353 HEALTH CARE ORGANIZATION, RISK MANAGEMENT & LIABILITY; 280-331 MANAGEMENT INFORMATION SYSTEMS; 280-211 FINANCIAL ACCOUNTING; 280-222 ORGANIZATIONAL BEHAVIOR; 619-354 HOSPITAL ORGANIZATION & MANAGEMENT; 619-401 EVALUATION OF HEALTH & SOCIAL SERVICE ORGANIZATIONS; 619-452 LEGAL ASPECTS OF HEALTH CARE; 272-423 PERSONNEL ADMINISTRATION; 619-352 DEPARTMENTAL MANAGEMENT IN HEALTH & SOCIAL SERVICES; 629-201 MACRO ECONOMICS; 629-202 MICRO ECONOMICS.

FIRST YEAR AMERICAN LAW COMPLETED
KENSINGTON UNIVERSITY COLLEGE OF LAW [unaccredited school]. [G.P.A. 3.0][COMPLETED IN U.S.A.][STATE APPROVED UNIV.]
[REGISTERED LAW STUDENT, STATE BAR OF CALIFORNIA, REG.#261753028].
COURSES COMPLETED: LL 500 LEGAL WRITING; LL 516 CRIMINAL LAW; LL 512 CONTRACTS; LL 514 TORTS; LL 529 SALES. FIRST YEAR BAR EXAM 24 JUNE, 1997 [CONFIRMATION LETTER 8 AUGUST, 1997].

MASTER OF ARTS [BEHAVIORAL SCIENCES DEPARTMENT]
SIMON FRASER UNIVERSITY, DEGREE DATED: MAY, 1975 [REGIONALLY ACCREDITED UNIVERSITY][G.P.A. 4.0][COMPLETED IN CANADA][EVALUATED TO U.S.A. EQUIVALENCY BY EDUCATIONAL RECORDS EVALUATION SERVICE, SACRAMENTO, CALIFORNIA][LETTER DATED 10 JANUARY, 1996, REFERENCE #95-01008][SIMON FRASER UNIVERSITY RANKING #1, FOR CANADIAN MEDIUM SIZED UNIVERSITIES, MACLEAN'S RANKINGS][LETTER OF RESEARCH BY: A.G. MOODIE, RESEARCH STUDIES & TESTING, BOARD OF SCHOOL TRUSTEES, DATED 16 APRIL, 1974][CONFIRMATION LETTER BY: A.G. MOODIE, RESEARCH STUDIES & TESTING, BOARD OF SCHOOL TRUSTEES, DATED 28 FEB., 1989]. BEHAVIORAL SCIENCES COURSES: CMNS 0800 CONTEMPORARY APPROACHES; CMNS 0801 METHODOLOGY & DESIGN; CMNS 0810 HUMAN FACTORS; CMNS 0820 INTERPERSONAL & GROUP PROCESSES; CMNS 0870 FIELD STUDY & CMNS 898 M.A. THESIS.

PUBLISHED MASTER'S THESIS ENTITLED: "THE MISSING PERSON IN MEASUREMENT TECHNIQUES OF INTERPERSONAL DISTANCE".

COPY APPEARS IN: NATIONAL LIBRARY OF CANADA, OTTAWA, CANADA. THESIS ON MICROFICHE: CALL #BF 469 M35 - AS044138; SUBJECTS - SPACE, INTERPERSONAL RELATIONS].

MASTER OF ARTS & PH.D. PSYCHOLOGY COURSES
AS INDEPENDENT STUDENT UNIVERSITY OF NEW BRUNSWICK [REGIONALLY ACCREDITED UNIVERSITY] & UNIVERSITY OF MANITOBA [REGIONALLY ACCREDITED UNIVERSITY][RESEARCH LETTER BY: DR. G.H. LOWTHER MB, CHB, MEDICAL SUPERINTENDENT, THE MANITOBA SCHOOL, 4 DECEMBER, 1972] [RESEARCH LETTER BY: MR. G.B. LITTLE, VICTORIA SCHOOL, DATED 5 APRIL, 1972][RESEARCH LETTER BY: DR. S.D. SINGH, MEERUT UNIVERSITY, DATED 1 NOVEMBER, 1977 & 17 JANUARY, 1978]
PSYCHOLOGY COURSES: PSYC 6031 ADVANCED STATISTICS; PSYC 6061 SOCIAL PSYCHOLOGY; PSYC 6051 PHYSIOLOGICAL PSYCHOLOGY; PSYC 0738 ADVANCED RESEARCH DESIGN; PSYC 0747 ADVANCED DEVELOPMENTAL PSYCHOLOGY; PSYC 0770 PROBLEMS IN PSYCHOLOGICAL RESEARCH I; PSYC 0772 PROBLEMS IN PSYCHOLOGICAL RESEARCH II; PSYC 0745 GROUP BEHAVIOUR; PSYC 0750 ADVANCED EXPERIMENTAL PSYCHOLOGY; PSYC 0810 SEMINAR ON DEVELOPMENTAL PSYCHOLOGY. TESTING EXPERIENCE: TEST OF NON-VERBAL INTELLIGENCE (T.O.N.I.); MINNESOTA MULTIPHASIC PERSONALITY INVENTORY (M.M.P.I.); SLOSSEN INTELLIGENCE TEST (S.I.T.); CALIFORNIA PSYCHOLOGICAL INVENTORY (C.P.I.); CAREER OCCUPATIONAL PREFERENCE SYSTEM (C.O.P.S.); SIXTEEN PERSONALITY FACTOR QUESTIONNAIRE (16 P.F.).

PH.D. COUNSELING PSYCHOLOGY
KENSINGTON UNIVERSITY [unaccredited school], DEGREE DATED: 26 AUGUST, 1994. [G.P.A. 3.83][COMPLETED IN U.S.A.][STATE APPROVED UNIVERSITY][REFERENCE LETTER BY: DR. WILLIAM KRAUS, DEAN OF FACULTY, DATED 24 AUGUST, 1994][REFERENCE LETTER BY: DR. JAMES LAMBERT, VICE PRESIDENT FOR ACADEMIC AFFAIRS, DATED 12 DEC., 1994].

HUMAN RESOURCES MANAGEMENT PROGRAM COURSES: KU 607 ORGANIZATION BEHAVIOR & MANAGEMENT; KU 516 PERSONNEL MANAGEMENT; KU698 DISSERTATION PROPOSAL.

COUNSELING PSYCHOLOGY COURSES: PSYC 573 PSYCHOPATHOLOGY; PSYC 522 PERSPECTIVES IN ETHOLOGY; PSYC 517 EDUCATIONAL PSYCHOLOGY; PSYC 587 SOCIAL PSYCHOLOGY; PSYC 556 DEPRESSION THEORY; PSYC 574 CHILD PSYCHOPATHOLOGY; PSYC 699 DISSERTATION.

TESTING EXPERIENCE: ADJECTIVE CHECK LIST (A.C.L.); CAREER ABILITY PLACEMENT SURVEY (C.A.P.S.); MASLACH BURNOUT INVENTORY (HUMAN SERVICES SURVEY); CHILD ANXIETY SCALE (C.A.S.); SLOSSON ORAL READING TEST (S.O.R.T.); CLINICAL ANALYSIS QUESTIONNAIRE (C.A.Q.); CANADIAN OCCUPATIONAL INTEREST INVENTORY (C.O.I.I.); MILLION CLINICAL MULTIAXIAL INVENTORY (M.C.M.I.); I.P.A.T. ANXIETY SCALE.

PUBLISHED DOCTORAL DISSERTATION ENTITLED: "INCIDENTS OF PHYSICAL ASSAULT AGAINST CHILD ABUSE INVESTIGATION WORKERS: THE NATURE OF CHILD-ABUSE PROTECTION LEGISLATION AS A POSSIBLE REASON FOR SUCH INCIDENTS: SOME CANADIAN AND AMERICAN EXAMPLES OF INTERNAL POLICIES ATTEMPTING TO DEAL WITH SUCH INCIDENTS: PLACING THE TREND OF SUCH INCIDENTS INTO A THEORETICAL PERSPECTIVE".

PROFESSIONAL EXPERIENCE OF TERRY W. MALLENBY:

NATIONAL DEFENSE RESEARCH, WESTWIN AIR FORCE BASE
["SECRET LEVEL" FEDERAL GOVERNMENT SECURITY CLEARANCE RECEIVED.,
MILITARY POLICE IDENTIFICATION; PASS # T 38793, DATED 15 MAY, 1972]. UNDER
A SUMMER TERM CONTRACT, GATHERED INFORMATION AND COMPLETED
DETAILED REPORT FOR THE RESEARCH DIRECTOR, DR. G.H.S. JONES, TRAINING
COMMAND HEADQUARTERS ON "THE RELATIVE EFFECTIVENESS OF
WHOLE- AND PART-TASK SIMULATORS", DATED 04 AUG., 1972.

CITY COLLEGE LECTURER, VANCOUVER CITY COLLEGE
[LETTER DATED 24 MARCH, 1974]. LECTURED IN ADULT INTEREST EVENING
COURSE ENTITLED: "VERBAL AND NON-VERBAL COMMUNICATION AT HOME AND
AT WORK".

FEDERAL MANPOWER & EMPLOYMENT COUNSELING
[CONFIRMATION LETTER DATED 24 MARCH, 1971][CONFIRMATION LETTER DATED
29 OCT., 1973]["SECRET LEVEL" SECURITY CLEARANCE RECEIVED][CONFIRMATION
MEMO DATED 05 APRIL, 1971] [CONFIRMATION MEMO DATED 06 DEC.,
1973][REFERENCE LETTER BY: MRS. LOIS CLARKE, CANADA MANPOWER &
IMMIGRATION, DATED 10 JUNE, 1975].

SPECIAL CLIENTS: DISADVANTAGED CLIENTS (DRUG, ALCOHOL, SUBSTANCE
ABUSE EMPLOYEES; PHYSICALLY AND MENTALLY HANDICAPPED WORKERS);
ARRANGING AND IMPLEMENTING ON-THE-JOB WORK CONTRACTS, INCLUDING
SIGNING AUTHORITY ON BEHALF OF THE DEPARTMENT FOR THE
IMPLEMENTATION AND PAYMENT OF SUCH CONTRACTS. ALSO: NORMAL DUTIES
OF A MANPOWER (EMPLOYMENT) COUNSELOR.

MEDIA ANNOUNCEMENTS: ANNOUNCED "JOB SHORTAGES" ON LOCAL T.V. &
RADIO PROGRAM WHILE AT DAWSON CREEK DISTRICT OFFICE.

TRAINING SESSIONS: CONDUCTED CREATIVE JOB SEARCH TECHNIQUES TRAINING
AND PRESENTATION [CONFIRMATION MEMO DATED 20 - 22 MARCH, 1974].

AGENCY PRESENTATIONS: PRESENTED TO ALLIED ASSOCIATIONS THE TYPE OF
SERVICES OFFERED BY THE DEPARTMENT [CONFIRMATION LETTER BY MS. A.M.
HILL DATED 15 MAY, 1974][CONFIRMATION LETTER BY S.L. WOLCH DATED 18
APRIL, 1974][CONFIRMATION LETTER BY S.L. WOLCH DATED 29 MAY, 1974].

COURSES COMPLETED: INDUSTRIAL TRAINING-SKILL SHORTAGES; TRAINING IN
INDUSTRY; OUTREACH AND LEAP PROJECTS; SPECIAL DIAGNOSTIC SERVICES;
IMMIGRATION SERVICES; ADULT BASIC EDUCATION PROGRAMS; MANPOWER
MOBILITY PROGRAMS; LABOR MARKET INFORMATION AND TRENDS;
INTERVIEWING TECHNIQUES; COUNSELING 101 AND 102 [CONFIRMATION MEMO
DATED 26 - 30 APRIL, 1971]; CLASSIFICATION AND DIRECTORY OF OCCUPATIONAL
CODES.

SUPREME COURT EXPERIENCE & TESTING EXPERIENCE: CONDUCTED G.A.T.B.
(GENERAL APTITUDE TEST BATTERY) TESTING; WAS "EXPERT WITNESS" IN

SUPREME COURT OF B.C. CASE GIVING TESTIMONY ON G.A.T.B. TESTING
COMPLETED, RE-TRAINING PROGRAMS AVAILABLE FOR ACCIDENT VICTIM
WORKER, WITH MARKET/LABOR TRENDS AND PROJECTED SALARY
[CONFIRMATION LETTER BY HOROWITZ & TICK, DATED 11 APRIL,
1974][CONFIRMATION LETTER BY ORECK, CHERNOFF & TICK, DATED 28 FEB., 1989]
.

STATE PROBATION SUPERVISION & PRE-DISPOSITION REPORTS*
[CERTIFICATE OF CONDUCT, ROYAL NEWFOUNDLAND CONSTABULARY,
CERTIFICATE DATED 04 FEB., 1994]. SUPERVISION OF PROBATION, COMMUNITY
SERVICE & COUNSELING OF YOUNG OFFENDERS.
YOUTH COURT EXPERIENCE: PRE-DISPOSITION REPORT PRESENTATIONS AT
YOUTH COURT.

*Newfoundland - The Lieutenant-Governor in Council may designate probation officers appointed
under the Department of Social Services Act to act as probation officers for the purposes of this
Act and may designate probation officers appointed under this Act to carry out the duties of
probation officers for the purposes of the Department of Social Services Act.

STATE CHILD PROTECTION & CHILD WELFARE SOCIAL WORKER
[CONFIRMATION LETTER 10 AUG., 1990][CONFIRMATION ASSESSMENT TO
PERMANENT STATUS DATED 11 MARCH, 1991][REFERENCE LETTER BY: MS.
KATHERINA LANZ, DATED 22 JUNE, 1990][REFERENCE LETTER BY: MR. DAVID R.
BUSSIERE, DATED 9 JULY, 1990]. INTAKE, INVESTIGATION AND ASSESSMENT OF
CHILD WELFARE/CHILD PROTECTION COMPLAINTS; JOINT INTERVIEWS WITH
R.C.M.P. RELATED TO CHILD SEXUAL/PHYSICAL ABUSE OR ASSAULT. FAMILY
COURT EXPERIENCE: PRESENTATION AT FAMILY COURT; COUNSELING FOR
CHILDREN SUBJECTED TO ABUSE, AS WELL AS COUNSELING FOR PARENT(S) AND
FAMILIES. DAY CARE INVESTIGATION & ASSESSMENT [CONFIRMATION LETTER 31
MARCH, 1992]. FOSTER HOME SUPERVISION & ASSESSMENT; INFANTS FOR
ADOPTION; CHANGE OF NAME ACT. COURSES COMPLETED: STPS #6000
UNDERSTANDING WIFE BATTERING COURSE [CONFIRMATION LETTER DATED 8
JANUARY, 1992].

FEDERAL CLASSIFICATION OFFICER MAXIMUM PRISON & PRE-PAROLE
[CONFIRMATION LETTER DATED 16 SEPTEMBER, 1974][SOLICITOR GENERAL
IDENTIFICATION PASS # 10631, DATED 04 SEPT., 1975]["SECRET LEVEL"
CLEARANCE REQUIRED AND RECEIVED, CONFIRMATION MEMO DATED 06 DEC.,
1973][SECURITY CLEARANCE CONFIRMATION LETTER, DATED 10 SEPT.,
1990][SECURITY CLEARANCE CONFIRMATION LETTER, DATED 16 NOV.,
1990][REFERENCE LETTER BY: MS. MARY STEINHAUSER MSW, CLASSIFICATION
OFFICER, DATED 2 APRIL, 1975][REFERENCE LETTER BY: W. MORT, DIRECTOR,
DATED 24 JULY, 1975][REFERENCE LETTER BY: W. ROMPF, SENIOR STAFFING
OFFICER, DATED 7 AUGUST, 1975][REFERENCE LETTER BY: R.E. WATKINS,
CLASSIFICATION SERVICES COORDINATOR, DATED 1 OCTOBER, 1975].

CASE MANAGEMENT: CLASSIFICATION OFFICER AT FEDERAL MAXIMUM
SECURITY PENITENTIARY RESPONSIBILITY FOR MAXIMUM SECURITY INMATES
(B.C. PENITENTIARY) AS WELL AS EXPERIENCE WITH MEDIUM
/MINIMUM/PROTECTIVE CUSTODY INMATES (MOUNTAIN PRISON), WITH

REPRESENTATION AND MEMBERSHIP PARTICIPATION ON INSTITUTIONAL WORK PLACEMENT BOARD, INTER- AND INTRA-REGIONAL TRANSFER BOARDS, PSYCHIATRIC AND CASE CONFERENCE BOARD, CLASSIFICATION BOARD.

PAROLE BOARD EXPERIENCE: INSTITUTIONAL REPRESENTATIVE AT THE NATIONAL PAROLE BOARD HEARINGS REGARDING PRE-PAROLE REPORTS.

CRIMINAL COURT EXPERIENCE: PRESENTATION AT CRIMINAL COURT. SUCCESSFUL CANDIDATE BILINGUAL CLASSIFICATION OFFICER [COMPETITION #75-CPS-PAC-IV-14; CONFIRMATION LETTER DATED 30 JANUARY, 1976].

HIGH RISK BONUS: RECEIVED PENNOLOGICAL FACTOR FOR FREQUENT CONTACT WITH MAXIMUM AND MEDIUM SECURITY FEDERAL INMATES (INCARCERATED FOR MORE THAN TWO YEARS)[CONFIRMATION MEMO DATED 20 JUNE, 1975].

COURSES COMPLETED: CANADIAN PENITENTIARY STAFF TRAINING SESSIONS AT STAFF TRAINING COLLEGE IN EDMONTON, ALBERTA 1974; DRUGS & YOUTH COUNSELING, DOUGLAS COLLEGE, 1975 [REFERENCE LETTER: R.E. WATKINS, CLASSIFICATION SERVICES COORDINATOR, DATED 1 OCTOBER, 1975]; HUMAN SOCIAL FUNCTIONING WORKSHOP TRAINING, 1975 [REFERENCE LETTER DATED 15 JANUARY, 1975].

STATE YOUNG OFFENDER RESIDENT UNIT SUPERVISOR [CONFIRMATION LETTER DATED 08 OCTOBER, 1992]. MANAGES ALL ASPECTS OF THE OPERATION OF A COTTAGE-BASED LIVING UNIT IN A LARGE SECURE CUSTODY AND REMAND FACILITY FOR YOUNG OFFENDERS.

ACTING DISTRICT MANAGER IN STATE SOCIAL SERVICES DEPARTMENT [CONFIRMATION E MAILS DATED 12 DEC., 1991; 09 DEC., 1991; 13 SEPT., 1991; 16 SEPT., 1991; 04 - 05 SEPT., 1991 & 21 - 22 - 23 JAN., 1992]. RESPONSIBLE FOR THE MANAGEMENT FRONT LINE SOCIAL WORK STAFF (CHILD WELFARE, CHILD PROTECTION, YOUTH CORRECTIONS, SOCIAL ASSISTANCE, SERVICES TO THE ELDERLY, REHABILITATIVE SERVICES, ADOPTION & POST ADOPTION, SERVICES TO THE MENTALLY & PHYSICALLY CHALLENGED, INDEPENDENCE PROGRAMS, ETC), FINANCIAL ASSISTANCE OFFICERS, CHILD MANAGEMENT SPECIALIST, COMMUNITY DEVELOPMENT WORKERS, CLERICAL AND SUPPORT STAFF IN A DISTRICT SOCIAL SERVICES OFFICE IN RURAL NEWFOUNDLAND, WITH A TERRITORY OF SOME 1500 SQUARE MILES. THOROUGH KNOWLEDGE OF THE CHILD WELFARE ACT, THE SOCIAL ASSISTANCE ACT, THE ADOPTION OF CHILDREN'S ACT, THE YOUNG OFFENDER'S ACT, ETC.,
INCLUDING ALL PROVINCIAL LEGISLATION, POLICY AND PROCEDURES RELATED TO ALL OF THE ABOVE NOTED PROGRAMS. KNOWLEDGE OF COLLECTIVE AGREEMENT.

OPERATIONS MANAGER SECURE CUSTODY YOUNG OFFENDER INSTITUTION [CONFIRMATION LETTER BY G. SKINNER DATED 16 MARCH, 1994][CONFIRMATION ASSESSMENT TO PERMANENT STATUS DATED 16 MARCH, 1994]. ADMINISTERS, DIRECTS AND MANAGES THE OVERALL FRONT LINE OPERATIONAL AND PROGRAM FUNCTIONS OF A LARGE PROVINCIAL SECURE CUSTODY AND REMAND FACILITY (WITH A COMPLEMENT OF 220 STAFF) FOR YOUNG OFFENDERS;

ENSURES THE MAINTENANCE OF PROPER PERSONNEL FUNCTIONS IN ACCORDANCE WITH POLICY AND PROCEDURES.

MANAGEMENT COURSES COMPLETED: EDP #3007 PREPARATION OF EVIDENCE [CONFIRMATION MEMO DATED 20 SEPT., 1993]; EFFECTIVE SUPERVISION [CONFIRMATION MEMO DATED 19 OCT., 1993 & DATED 23 NOV., 1993]; LABOR RELATIONS & THE LINE MANAGER [CONFIRMATION MEMO DATED 04 NOV., 1993]; LEADERSHIP & MOTIVATION [CONFIRMATION MEMO DATED 06 JAN., 1994]; EFFECTIVE MANAGEMENT [CONFIRMATION MEMO DATED 10 JAN., 1994]; MANAGING CONFLICT [CONFIRMATION MEMO DATED 11 JAN., 1994]; PROBLEM SOLVING [CONFIRMATION MEMO DATED 18 JAN., 1994]; CONDUCTING EFFECTIVE MEETINGS [CONFIRMATION MEMO DATED 10 JAN., 1994].

FIRST AID & EMERGENCY SCENE MANAGEMENT COURSES: FIRST AID TRAINING [CONFIRMATION MEMO DATED 10 MAY, 1994]; EMERGENCY SCENE MANAGEMENT -ARTIFICIAL RESPIRATION; CHOKING -WOUNDS & BLEEDING; SHOCK, UNCONSCIOUSNESS & FAINTING; JOINT INJURIES, STRAINS & RESCUE CARRIES; MULTIPLE INJURY MOVEMENT -HEART ATTACK & STROKE; ONE-RESCUER CPR [CERTIFICATE TO HEART SAVER LEVEL]; MEDICAL CONDITIONS [DIABETES, EPILEPSY, CONVULSIONS & ALLERGIES; ST. JOHN'S AMBULANCE CERTIFICATE: SAFETY ORIENTED FIRST AID: STANDARD LEVEL: ELECTIVE MODULES - 06, 08, 12, 13, 18, 19, 20, 21.

OTHER COURSES COMPLETED: INTRODUCTION TO COMPUTER BASICS: PARTS I & II; UNDERSTANDING DOS -WINDOWS 3.1; FILE MANAGER -UNDERSTANDING NETWORKS; WORDPERFECT 5.2 -MS MAIL -MS SCHEDULE; [CONFIRMATION LETTER DATED 29 DECEMBER, 1993][CONFIRMATION CERTIFICATE DATED FALL, 1993/WINTER, 1994].

COURT EXPERIENCE: SUBPOENA TO WITNESS, SUPREME COURT, DATED 1993; SUBPOENA TO WITNESS, STATE COURT, 1993.